HOW TO BE
A PERSONAL STORY MENTOR

HOW TO BE
A PERSONAL STORY MENTOR

Helping People Connect the Dots of Their Lives Using the StoryQ Method

by Dr. Rick Stevenson

StoryQ Publishers
Seattle, Washington

Published by StoryQ Publishers, an imprint of

Methow Press
P.O. Box 1213, Twisp, WA 98856
http://www.methowpress.com

Printed in the United States of America.

ISBN 13: 979-8-9913567-3-2

DEDICATION

This book is dedicated to everyone who has courageously helped to develop the StoryQ Method over the last quarter of a century via 7000 in-person interviews and 500,000 automated iOS app interviews. Like a fine wine, longitudinal projects only grow richer with time. So, infinite thanks to:

- The kids and adults who have laid bare their vulnerabilities by doing the hard work to discover and share their stories while collectively growing this grand experiment;

- The parents who have entrusted us with the confidential lives and emotional development of their children;

- The schools, businesses, and organizations which have seen the value of this method and advocated for it;

- The individuals and grantors who have generously given to it;

- The mental health professionals and mentors who have shared the best of their knowledge and experience in helping to create the Method;

- My partners including Max, Angelique, Greg, Brendan, Teri, and several others who have invested their time and energies in this project; and

- The members of my family, who have given me their wisdom, experience, support, and patience as the ambitions for this Method only grow day by day.

Rick Stevenson
Seattle, January 1, 2025

TABLE OF CONTENTS

I have a nephew named Andy.

I was staying with his family when he asked me if he could audition for the 5000 Days Project—the documentary project that has led to me doing more than 7000 interviews with kids over six continents and inspired a new method of interviewing.

So, I sat down in front of the camera, as I had done earlier with his older brother and sister, and he immediately burst into tears…

I said, "Andy, are you okay? I haven't even asked you a question yet." He nodded and said, "I know, but I know what you're going to ask me." I said, "Oh, yeah? What's that?" He replied, "You're going to ask me about the last time I cried and why." I nodded and said, "Well, that's normally question seven, but it sounds like you already know the answer to that question."

He nodded with tears dripping onto his lap. He took a deep breath then proceeded to tell me about an event that had happened three days before in his classroom. He had been cast in the school play and the teacher asked him to stand and sing his solo in front of the class. As he tried to continue, he broke down again crying.

I looked at him, feeling his pain, and told him to take his time. I wanted to hear the story when he was ready to tell it. He took a deep breath and tried again but the tears kept

The 5000 Days Project, Andy, Age 9

flowing. Finally, on the third attempt, Andy was able to get the story out. Basically, what happened was that he stood up, sang his solo, the kids laughed at him, and he ran out of the classroom in tears—the sort of childhood experience that would put you in therapy in your 40s as to why you are afraid to speak in front of the Rotary Club.

Just for stupid filmmaker reasons, I asked him if he'd tell the story again loud and clear so that I could get it all on film. He did so and had no trouble getting through it. Suddenly, I got an idea. I asked Andy if he trusted me. He said, "Of course." I said, "Okay, last time. I promise. I want you to tell me the story one last time, but this time I want you to sing it." He looked at me strangely then shrugged and started to sing his story. "I was in my class and the teacher asked me to sing my solo…" In a moment he was laughing.

Loudly. At himself. And at the absurdity of the situation.

And this is when I saw, firsthand, the value of verbal journaling—the potential the interview process held for all of us. In a very short time, I watched Andy take an event that was so difficult for him that he could not even get it out of his mouth… and I watched him barf up his story, hold it in his hand, expose it to the healing qualities of the air, and laugh at it.

For you biblical scholars out there, do you remember the first instruction God reportedly gave Adam and Eve? God instructed them to name the animals because, according to ancient Hebrew tradition, naming something gave you power over it.

Consider another example from the 5000 Days Project. (See the link below for further details.)

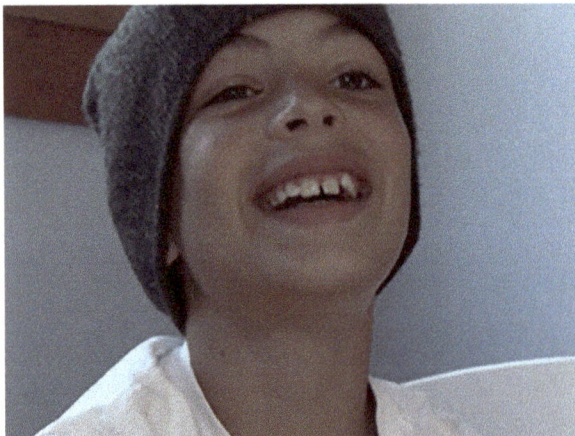

The 5000 Days Project, Andy, Age 9

Take time to watch clips of Kayden and Isaac (right) using this QR code.

tinyurl.com/storyq01

Dr. Rick Stevenson

"Verbal journaling is more effective because emotions which are orally expressed start to lose power over us."

These two boys, just like Andy, discovered that when they named their issues, they could gain power over them.

From a physiological perspective, how does that work?

The brain science behind this makes perfect sense. There is a decades-old history of evidence surrounding the benefits of journaling. But I've witnessed time and time again that verbal journaling, based on our age-old oral tradition of telling stories face-to-face, is even more effective because emotions that are verbally expressed start to lose power over us. A brain imaging study by Dr. Matt Leiberman of UCLA has proved that by verbalizing our feelings of sadness, anger and pain become less intense. As Dr. Lea Waters explains, "As soon as you ask a child to verbalize their emotion, the child accesses their brain's prefrontal cortex, which is the part they use for language and to process what's happening. It takes them out of their amygdala, the lower part of the brain which is responsible for those strong emotional reactions, and helps them calm down because it controls their impulses."

I am grateful that you are interested in learning The Art of Personal Story Mentoring. I believe helping individuals of all ages to tell their story is among the noblest of pursuits for reasons we will discover. And in that discovery, I think you will see how it can be a key to a brighter future for all of us.

The 5000 Days Project, Kayden & Isaac, Age 10

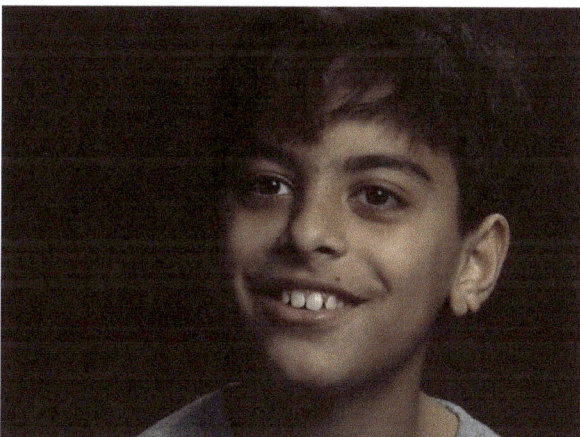

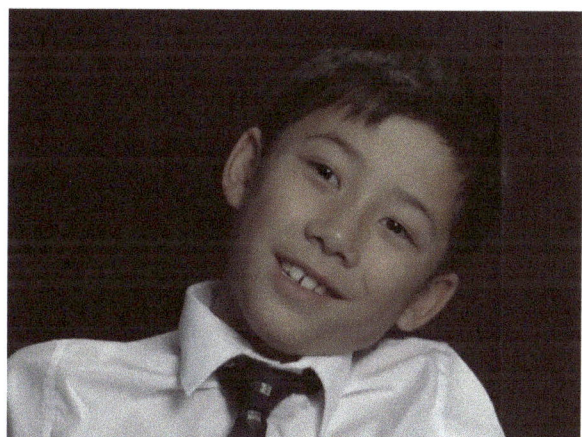

Welcome to this journey.

I'm Rick Stevenson, and this is *How to Be a Personal Story Mentor: Helping People Connect the Dots of Their Lives Using the StoryQ Method.*

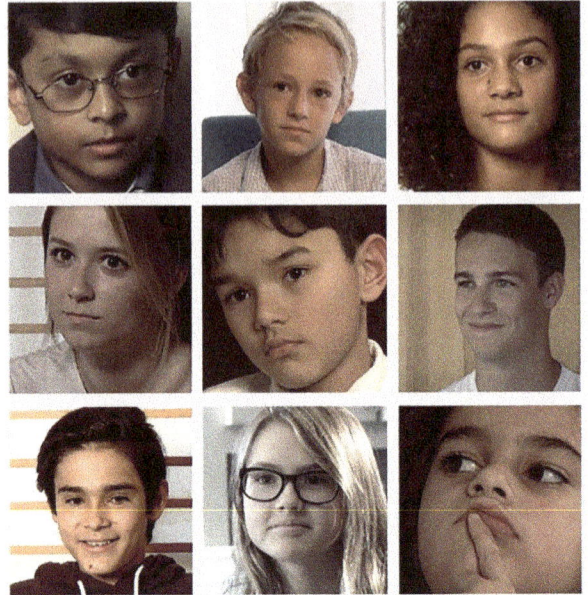

.

Dr. Rick Stevenson

When people hear the word "interview," they often get this nervous feeling in their stomach.

There's the job interview when you have a lot at stake and want to make the perfect impression…

And then there's the "documentary or journalistic interview" that is designed to provoke people into telling some truth—often one they don't want to tell.

Both forms of interviews are important in their own ways. Both are designed to serve the interviewer—to get what they need or want. As a result, both cause stress and both have casualties. Neither is acceptable when you've been entrusted with the privilege of helping someone—especially children—find their authentic story.

I'd like you to imagine another type of interview, which is dedicated solely to serving the interviewee, where there are only winners and the effects can be cumulative and life-changing. In fact, I would argue that when an atmosphere of trust is established, truths can be revealed that will benefit both the interviewer and the interviewee.

This is the kind of interview for which I'm preparing you. This is about the interviewer being a facilitator of self-realization and growth, whether it be for children, teens, or

The 5000 Days Project, Arianne / Matthew / Kai Yee

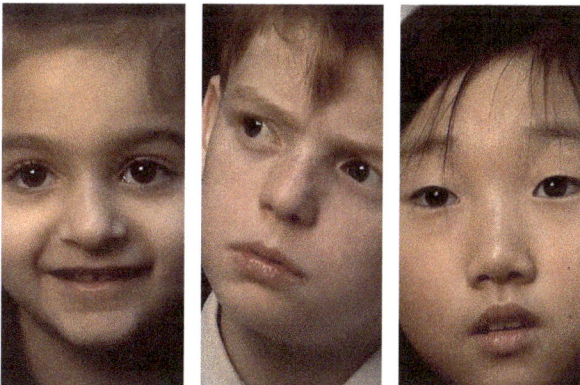

Scan the QR code for *Three Different Kids*, an example from one school in Canada.

tinyurl.com/storyq02

adults. If you complete this training, you may qualify to become a certified Personal Story Mentor using the StoryQ Method. This allows you to help others learn to tell the most difficult story they'll ever tell—their own. You will help them grow their emotional intelligence (EQ), heal some of their emotional wounds, and help them answer their greatest mystery: Who in the world am I?

This approach, of course, comes from Socrates, the father of Western philosophy, the ultimate questioner of everyone and everything. Born in 469 BC, he was a central part of the golden age of Pericles' Athens, and his belief in the value of verbal inquiry is evidenced by the fact that he never authored any texts. His enormous influence was exerted by the works of his students which included Plato and Xenophon... and beyond through such philosophers as Kierkegaard and Nietzsche.

"Each of us owns nothing more valuable than our own story and, if we learn to tell it, we unlock a deep well of human wisdom within ourselves."

Socrates believed that wisdom began with the admission of one's own ignorance, and felt an unexamined life was not worth living. He sought to move beyond strictly theological interpretations of right and wrong and felt that reason and ethics could guide us. Most fundamentally, he believed that happiness could be achieved by humans through simply

Socrates, Plato, Xenophon, Kierkegaard, Nietzsche

Dr. Rick Stevenson

knowing themselves better. The method you are about to learn owes pretty much everything to this tradition.

The main difference—or more accurately *addition*—to this approach involves storytelling. Instead of a philosophical or psychological inquiry, the StoryQ Method employs the most familiar, friendly, and effective means of human communication—a particular type of storytelling. Personal Storytelling.

In fact, after conducting more than 7000 interviews, I have come to believe that each of us owns nothing more valuable than our own story. If we learn to tell it, we unlock a deep well of human wisdom within ourselves, wisdom that can lead us to discovering our better selves and a better world.

So how did all of this happen?

Well, in the next lesson, I will tell you another story.

LESSON TWO: THE STORYQ METHOD ORIGIN STORY

Over the last two decades, I have conducted over 7000 interviews with kids across six continents. It happened largely by mistake.

It all began when I was seven years old and held a huge crush on Jackie Kennedy. Yes, she was our First Lady, and yes, she was 25 years and 360 days older than me—but who's counting? And yes, she was married to that JF… whatever guy. It didn't matter; I thought she was the perfect woman! I know this fascination with romance was fostered by my parents' amazing love story involving three chance meetings against the epic backdrop of the Second World War. From an early age, all I wanted was to find the right person and have a family.

Cut to 30 years later… and I was no closer to finding the right person than I had been when I was seven. My then girlfriend of three years insisted we go into therapy and find out why I couldn't commit. I replied that therapy was for people with problems. She gave me "the look" and I said, "Okay." Well, three weeks later we broke up and I got to keep the therapist, Donna. And thankfully over the next few months, Donna asked me all of the right questions to help me discover that the problem was not the people I was meeting, it was me. Boom! This was probably painfully obvious to those around me—but had never occurred to me. I had spent years looking for the right person instead of becoming the right person. And that revelation was freeing because if the

Rick, Max, Madee, Julie, Oliver, Leah

problem was me, then I could do something about it. And that's what I did.

As I began to figure myself out, I met Julie—and thankfully was able to recognize the woman of my dreams that was right before me!

She came pre-packaged with Max and Madee, and then we had our son Oliver and adopted daughter Leah. After having spent two decades producing, directing, and writing films everywhere but home, I decided to safeguard this precious relationship by starting a project that would keep me with my family in Seattle. It became the 5000 Days Project—which is roughly the time it takes to go through school—and it would be a longitudinal documentary with me interviewing kids once a year as they grow up, creating the ultimate portrait of childhood.

Dr. Rick Stevenson

The first interview was in February 2001, and the next was in December 2001. What happened in between, however, was 9/11. Suddenly I realized the kids desperately wanted and needed to talk on a much much deeper level because the world had gone crazy around them. It was then that the project took a dramatic turn. Instead of being just a documentary, the priority became helping each kid figure out their place in the world.

Working with my brain scientist friend, Dr. John Medina, author of *Brain Rules*, and a bevy of experienced psychologists, counselors, and teachers, I developed the StoryQ Method which flipped the interview on its head. With the StoryQ technique, it ceased being about making documentaries… though we still make them. It became primarily focused on the needs of the child—or person of any age—being interviewed. It became nourishing and full of discovery, helping the individual in self-

Books by Dr. John Medina

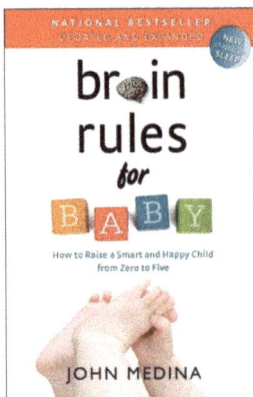

Learn more about Dr. John Medina's *Brain Rules* by using this QR code.

tinyurl.com/storyq03

"If each of us owns nothing more valuable than our own story, is there anything more important than finding out what it is?"

discovery by realizing the power of their own story.

Unlike the "job" or "journalistic" interview, there are no casualties in this process. There are just people who will likely emerge with the skill to tell the most difficult story they'll ever tell—their own.

Think about it. If each of us owns nothing more valuable than our own story, is there anything more important than finding out what it is?

This experience has changed my life in all sorts of wonderful ways. First, I know I've filled a need because, beyond a caring parent or teacher, most kids have precious few people willing to truly listen to them, ask them the big key-life questions, and give them honest feedback. Obviously, when kids get that, they have a much better chance of becoming fully-functioning adults.

Second, if this project is about helping kids, teens, and adults solve the greatest mystery they'll ever face, namely, "Who in the world am I?," you'll be excited to know that the benefit goes both ways. With each interview, I am constantly learning more and more about myself… and you will too. Why? I'm convinced that while we may reach the legal age of adulthood, large parts of our emotional

StoryQ Global Reach

Over 500,000 **StoryQ** videos collected

selves are still stuck in various stages of arrested development. And when you are constantly exposed to the challenges of being a kid and then you bring your current perspective to it, revelation after revelation occurs. It's truly a win/win as a StoryQ Personal Story Mentor. When my wife, Julie, pointed out how much I grow emotionally with each season of interviews, it suddenly occurred to me, "Oh, my gosh, have I got several hundred kids around the world helping me work out my own issues with arrested development?" The answer is, well, probably. Yes!

For this reason, while our initial focus was on kids and teens, the lessons learned from these interviews made us much more effective interviewers of adults. Even when you are interviewing someone in their eighties, if you can find the child within you are most likely to find the source of most of their longings and their fears. Hence, while many of the experiences and lessons shared in this book deal with children and teens, many are not only relevant to adults but essential to understanding them.

THE STORYQ METHOD INSPIRATION

When I was a child, my favorite book was Crockett Johnson's *Harold and the Purple Crayon*.

The plot was simple. Harold, a cartoon boy in footie PJs, lies in bed one night and sees the moon shining through his window. He decides to have an adventure, so he picks up his purple crayon... but suddenly realizes he does not know where to go. So Harold draws a road and follows it. At some point his hand grows unsteady, drawing ripples, and he falls into a vast ocean of his own making. He does not know how to swim, so he quickly draws

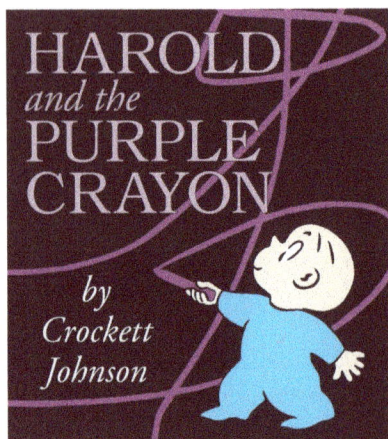

> ## "Emotions hold vital clues to what is right and wrong within us. They are our early warning system."

himself a boat and gets on board. However, the boat will not move, so he draws a sail. Soon he is headed back toward shore where, tired and hungry, he draws himself a tree to create shade, as well as a number of pies to eat. And so on.

Only years later did I realize why *Harold and the Purple Crayon* was my favorite childhood book: Harold realized that he was the author of his own story and proceeded to use his crayon to (literally) illustrate that point.

The world is split in two. There are those immobilized by a grievance mentality—those who lack the knowledge or courage to pick up the crayon; they pass the authorship of their story to others and end up being a secondary character in someone else's story. Then there are those who pick up the crayon and assume authorship; they have the courage and curiosity to seek answers to the single greatest mystery in their life: "Who in the world am I?"

We designed the StoryQ Method with this goal in mind: To help individuals recognize that they are holding the crayon—that with every thought, every word, every deed, every action, every moment of every day, they are writing their autobiography, in real time.

So how is this best achieved?

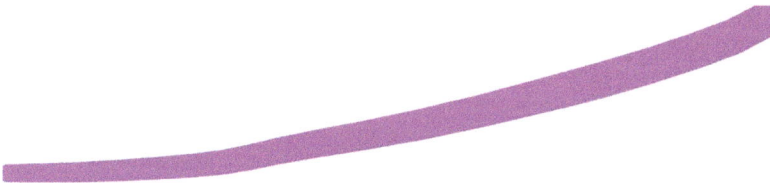

The StoryQ Method is all about allowing individuals to discover their own truth by learning to tell their own stories. Through a guided, neo-Socratic inquiry, individuals can access an inherent wisdom within that can start to heal the grand majority of our emotional wounds and make us high-functioning and healthy adults. As I have mentioned in connection with our Lessons, we might liken this to a type of "emotional immune system" that, unlike its physiological counterpart, is not triggered by trauma but by emotional intelligence and awareness of trauma and its effects.

While many of us find our emotions confusing if not frightening, those very emotions actually hold vital clues to what is right and wrong within us. They are our early warning system. Our brains tell us whatever we want to believe but our emotions quite simply are just what they are. The good news is that, by learning how to read and process them, we can solve many of our own mysteries. The StoryQ Method is basically about asking the right questions in the right order, at the right time, and in the right setting to help the interviewees discover their own right answers.

For a five-minute primer on the StoryQ Method, use this QR code .

tinyurl.com/storyq04

On December 26th, 2004, an uneducated aboriginal elder was standing on the shore of a remote island in the Indian Ocean. He noticed the strange movement of the tides, the stillness in the air, the way the monkeys and birds were behaving… and he recalled oral stories that had been passed down for generations. He got his people to high ground, and not one life was lost—unlike the quarter of a million others who tragically perished in that infamous Boxing Day Tsunami. Why do we tell stories? We tell stories because they save our lives in countless ways.

Storytelling is the basis of all human communication and connection. According to the long-running study on happiness at Harvard University, connection—not wealth, education, or position—is ultimately what gives us meaning. That is why storytelling, the oldest of human traditions starting with cave drawings and sharing around campfires under a canopy of stars, is key to our well-being.

By teaching our kids to tell the most difficult story they'll ever tell—their own—we give them the ability to develop the tools to tell *any* story. Learning to tell stories is perhaps the most essential skill they can develop. Why? Because all of business, education, law, science —everything is centered around storytelling. Even math is storytelling because numbers are only made meaningful when a story is attached. Twelve—a dozen eggs, a jury for

— The 5000 Days Project, Phanit (Cambodia)

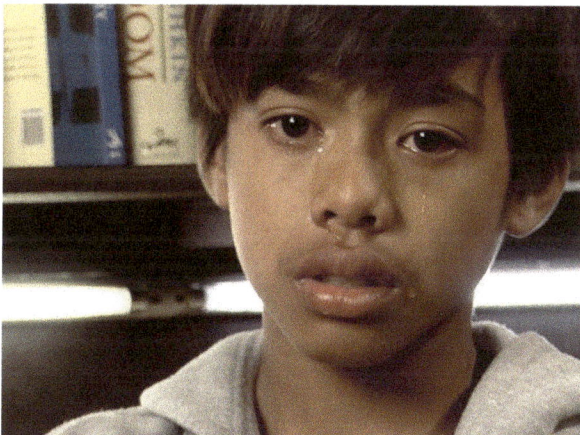

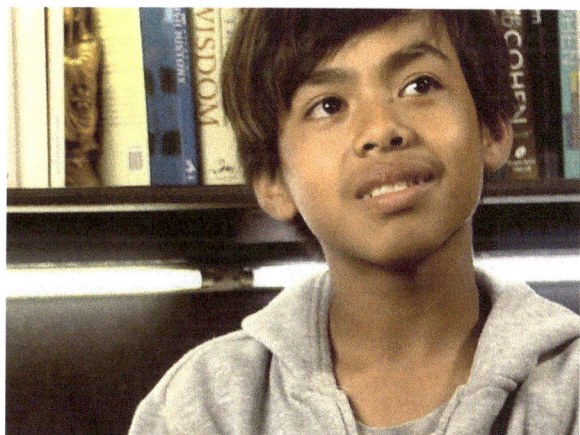

> ## "All of human communication is storytelling. It's the currency of human connectedness. It is primeval. It's in our very DNA."

Dr. Rick Stevenson

justice, twelve Thai boys caught in a cave. All of human communication is storytelling. It's the currency of human connectedness. It is primeval. It's in our very DNA.

And teaching our kids to tell their own story is essential because their personal stories matter. If you think about it, our story is our one fundamental contribution to humanity. We are born and we immediately start talking. We take air, we take food, we take space. What do we have to *leave* but our story? Amazingly, the United Nations estimates that as many as a third of all babies are never even registered as being born. If you live and die and there's no record of you having existed, what does that say about our failure to recognize the value of the human story? If a tree falls in the forest and nobody is there to hear it… does it make a sound?

There's an African proverb that says when an old person dies, a library burns down. If you think about it both in economic and moral terms, what a tragic waste of human capital. Think of the knowledge and experience we lose daily—knowledge and experience we could use to improve or save lives. Knowledge and experience that could help us avoid repeating past mistakes. Knowledge and experience that could give us a true picture of

humanity—not just part of it. J. R. R. Tolkien, in one of his lesser known works, metaphorically envisioned all of humanity as a grand choir that only reached sonic perfection when *every* voice could be heard. Just imagine…

Finally, learning to tell our own story is the key to a better world. Near the end of my interviews, I ask the question "What are your three wishes?" The majority of kids ask for "world peace"—that is, up until twelve years old. After that, the wish starts to sound naive to them. Having written a book on world peace for my doctorate, I know how elusive a political, economic, or social solution can be. But the good news is that when we learn to tell our own stories, we can make progress toward that elusive goal. For instance, stories can be used to combat the ignorance and fear that fuel conflict and war. When we connect with our enemies as humans instead of as faceless groups to be feared, we realize that we all share a common burden as human beings. To paraphrase Sting, "Our enemies love their children too."

Beyond this, when it comes to our own role in creating world peace, it was the ancient Chinese philosopher Lao Tzu who refused to let any of us off the hook. To paraphrase, he said, "There will never be peace between nations until there is peace within nations, there will never be peace within nations until there is peace between neighbors, there will never be peace between neighbors until there is peace within families, and there will never be peace within families until there is peace within our own hearts."

In other words, if we each take care of making the content of our own stories the best it can be, we can change our world from the ground up. In this way each of our stories is epic and

— *Lao Tzu*

essential. It's why our story is the most valuable thing we own and why it's the key to a better world—something each of us can make happen. So *that* is why our mission here is noble and important.

Emotions. For better or for worse, we all have them. At times we love them, at times we hate them. Often we are embarrassed by them. In fact, all three reactions—love, hate, and embarrassment—are emotions that come from the same place: a tiny almond-shaped part of our brain called the "amygdala."

Now, this often unwelcome and embarrassing visitor is actually our best friend because it has helped us to survive. When we stepped out of our cave for a morning stretch and found a hangry predator waiting impatiently for its next meal, it was the amygdala that went into "fight or flight" mode and gave us a chance to survive. When we get too close to the edge of a tall building or we're about to give a public speech, it's the amygdala that sends our stomachs into our throats, alerting us to potential danger of death… or worse, public embarrassment. Or when we feel love or start to fall in love, it's the amygdala that triggers those chemicals in our bodies that give us that one-of-a-kind feeling.

Of course, not all fears are worthy of the importance the amygdala gives them, just as not all feelings of attraction are based in reality. And it's the imbalance or lack of predictability that leads us to distrust and feel threatened by this impetuous friend. That is why we need to learn emotional regulation, which is achieved when we know ourselves well enough to balance those signals from the

The amygdala is about the size of a shelled peanut

amygdala with reason based in our prefrontal lobe. That process, when added to experience, contributes to emotional well-being and stability.

All of that said, we as humans have so dramatically overreacted to this process that we often try to shut out emotions for fear of what they might do to us. And while all of our emotions might not always be based in reality, they are based 100% in *our* reality—and understanding our reality first is the only way to solve any given personal problem. For instance, men are often so frightened by their emotions that they consider it "masculine" to discount them altogether. But when a boy of ten who is experiencing some big feelings is told to "man up" by his father or other father figures, what message are we as role models sending to him? We're telling him that his emotions should be discounted, that they are not real or cannot be trusted.

We're telling him that the one thing that will tell him the complete truth of what's going on inside needs to be ignored. The same thing is true with a girl whose "big feelings" are discounted as being the product of hormones or "female irrationality."

Throughout Western and Eastern literature, our heroes are often the lone, courageous individuals who suffer silently in the face of great pain. They are resilient. They are non-complainers. They personify strength and courage. Or do they? While resilience and mindset are keys to survival and characteristics to be admired, in isolation they come at a price.

Every day we take bullets—disappointments, failures, criticisms, betrayals. The list goes on. If we don't take the time to process those feelings, to operate on those bullets, by the time we're adults our bodies are riddled with

Dr. Rick Stevenson

Achilles facing off with Hector in Greek heroic tradition

20

> # "If knowledge is power, self-knowledge is *super* power."

bullets. No wonder there is so much mental illness and outright pain in our society.

I recently interviewed a kid whose family was breaking up. This kid was courageous and fearless as an athlete. She would perform daring feats without a second thought about the potential for injury. However, when it came to talking about her feelings, all of that courage disappeared. She became paralyzed by the fear.

I am excited to teach you how to help interviewees of any age to open up and confront their fears—because the more they define and confront their fears, the more they gain power over them and the less those fears will define them. But that takes courage—in fact, that takes rewriting the very definition of courage. Courage is not the stiff-upper-lip tradition of pretending not to feel pain—even though that is sometimes required in the short-term. Courage is confronting our pain and processing it. It starts with understanding the DNA of our emotions.

Our bodies are extraordinary machines. Our natural immune system attacks life-threatening diseases or viruses and heals all sorts of physical wounds. As previously stated, I think we also have a type of an emotional immune system. However, unlike our physical immune system which kicks in automatically, this "emotional immune system" is only unlocked by self-knowledge. Self-knowledge is achieved by acknowledging and under-standing our emotions. That is why our

Visit the National Alliance on Mental Illness (NAMI) using this QR code.

tinyurl.com/storyq05

emotions are actually our best friends. They are a divining rod to the truth. That is why I feel that if knowledge is power, self-knowledge is *super* power. That is why the ultimate goal is to arm each interviewee with their own superpower.

Later on, we're going to dissect some of the scenarios you'll run up against in helping an interviewee deal with sadness, fear, anger, and disappointment—the rogues' gallery of unwelcomed emotions. But in the meantime, suffice it to say that encouraging an interviewee to explore and embrace their emotions is the key to everything. To that end, I'll recommend at some stage of the interview giving them an EQ Test. Stay tuned!

LESSON FIVE: PREPARING OURSELVES—THE ROLE OF OUR OWN EMOTIONS

You may recall from Lesson Two the story of my own emotional awakening after the well-deserved smackdown from my girlfriend of three years. We go into couples therapy—or else. So we went, and three weeks later, we were broken up. And I got to keep the therapist. Donna.

Over the next six months Donna helped me unpack my past via Family of Origin therapy and discover the problems I had making a commitment. In short, I had grown up an extremely sensitive and creative little boy with a big temper. But as I turned ten and then eleven, my temper became no longer appropriate. I was taught to pack it away. This was especially important because my very

WASPish family put a priority on harmony which, I soon learned, was more important than the truth. This had been passed down to my parents from their parents and so on. So I learned that, in my most intimate relationships, it was inappropriate to express what I truly felt. Hence, whenever I developed an intimate relationship, intuitively I felt my true self become threatened. My fear was that a life-long relationship meant I would not be allowed to be myself.

Furthermore, conflict represented failure in our family. Shouting was the ultimate sin. Astoundingly, not once did I hear my parents fight. Though they had an amazing love story, it took me years to realize that arguing could

The Stevenson Family (ca. 1978)

be a healthy way to negotiate differences, and that their relationship was extremely rare.

For instance, one month before our breakup, my girlfriend and I had agreed to invite an eleven-year-old friend to live with us at the request of his single mother who was having trouble with him. His mother was this brilliant, beautiful, and passionate woman whose temper could ignite a thunderstorm. Her equally brilliant and passionate son had inherited these qualities and so a break seemed in order. Of course less than a month later, my girlfriend of three years and I had broken up and suddenly, when this boy arrived, I immediately became a single father. This boy's own father had not been much a part of his life, so he welcomed male influence in his matriarchal family and I got my first chance to be a father figure.

Over their six-month separation, this boy and his mother had numerous conflicts on the phone culminating in him not wanting to go back home at the mutually agreed-upon time. Being equally good friends with both of them, I was constantly trying to calm the anger expressed in their shouting matches. Being a peacemaker between these two passionate people became my role. During one of my own therapy sessions, I told Donna of this situation and she hit me with an unexpected question. She asked, "Rick, what are you doing in their relationship? They have one, and you have one with each one of them. But why have you inserted yourself in between them? That's for them to figure out."

I immediately jumped to defend myself saying I was just trying to be a peacemaker. She asked me why. I replied, "Because it seems like the way I can most help them. It just hurts to see two people I care about misunderstand each other so badly that they shout at each other."

Eirine, the Greek ideal for peacemakers

> "We not only need to take this medicine before we prescribe it to others, we also need to learn from the personal revelations it brings about."

She replied, "I trust that your intentions are pure but they are also complicated. For instance, at what age did your family shut down your feelings for fear of conflict?"

Boom! Oh my gosh, Donna was right. Despite my seemingly well-intentioned peacemaking, much of it was about my own discomfort with conflict. I was trying to impose on them the same thing that had been emotionally constipating me. I immediately pulled myself out of the equation and let son and mother figure it out themselves—which they're still doing, with love, decades later.

It was at that point that I suddenly realized there is no such thing as an objective participant in any relationship—even between an interviewer and an interviewee. Our views and behaviors will always be colored by our past experiences. So what can we do to address that truth?

Two things. First, we can develop our self-awareness to the point where we are aware of our influences and how they prejudice our point of view. To that end, I recommend that each of us find a partner who can interview us with some of the suggested items in Lesson Ten: The Questions.

Many complex equations cannot be solved by "u"

$$ax + by + cz = d$$
$$ex + fy + gz = h$$
$$ix + jy + kz = l$$

Just to warn you, my oldest son challenged me to do this exercise and I was sobbing by question three. When my son asked to interview me, I discovered that we not only need to take this medicine before we prescribe it, but we need to learn from the personal revelations it brings about. And this especially involves the conscious identification of our own personal fears.

For instance, most of us have a fear of rejection. Who wants it? Who needs to put themselves through it? So here is a precise example of how our fears might influence our interview technique.

On the left is my son Oliver at seven—innocent, inquisitive, enthusiastically embracing the world. And on the right you see him at fourteen, a bit sour-faced, cynical, and unsure about the world. The most common comment I get from parents of teenagers is, "I'm not sure he's going to want to talk. He doesn't want to talk about anything these days."

While it is true that part of being a teenager is developing your own private life as you separate from your parents, I have seldom met a teen who did not want to talk—deep down—whether they consciously realized it or not. It's our job as interviewers to push through the wall and connect simply as two humans with mutual respect. The entire secret to interviewing kids is to treat them with the respect you'd treat another adult. And the entire secret to interviewing adults is to not be afraid to talk to the kid that still resides within them. As for interviewing teens, more often than not, when we tell ourselves that our teen does not want to talk, we are projecting our own insecurities and fears of rejection onto them. It's that fear that creates the gulf between adults and teenagers.

Oliver Stevenson at 7, and at 14

Watch the time-lapse face-morph of Oliver Stevenson using this QR code

tinyurl.com/storyq06

Dr. Rick Stevenson

"Become the best version of yourself and bring it to your work."

Second, as Lao Tzu suggested, the very best thing you can do for each person you interview, and for the world in general, is to become the best version of yourself and bring it to your work. It sounds kind of corny but it's true. When you are in a bad place, it will be more difficult for you to help guide your interviewee to a good place. The more you master your fears and bring your good self to the table, the more your interviewee will trust you and the more good you can do for them.

If emotions reveal the truth of what's going on inside of us, measuring Emotional Intelligence (the EQ) is the key to solving our greatest individual mystery: "Who in the world am I?" Add that to the Positive Education animation (see below) and you discover that Emotional Intelligence is actually the key to pretty much everything—including maximizing your IQ. Again, it's not our brain that wants to learn, it's our emotions.

So, try this on yourself as well as your interviewees. Say: "Cavemen had two emotions. 'Me feel good. Me feel bad.' You're not a caveman. You have many more emotions, and the more you can name them and identify where they came from, the higher your EQ (the emotional/psychological version of your IQ). So, let's test your EQ."

You then proceed to give them a story-based challenge. Challenge them to name and source as many emotions as possible since the point of waking up yesterday morning to the current moment, today. Give them a few minutes to write them down. Then have them share the list. If I'm speaking before a group, I may share my own: "I woke up being excited about my trip but also hesitant because I never like leaving my family. Next, I felt relaxed as I showered and shaved but as I ran through my speech and stumbled over a couple passages, I felt nervous that I might screw up. Why nervous? Because it means a lot to me to do

Rick speaking at a Positive Education conference in Australia

Watch Part 1 of our video series on Positive Education using this QR code.

tinyurl.com/storyq07

"As you ask them to identify their feelings and why they had them, you can see self-knowledge grow before your eyes."

Dr. Rick Stevenson

the best job possible. Not to mention I fear failure and humiliation." Okay, excitement, regret, relief, anxiety, and passion—and all before breakfast.

I've actually done this while speaking to business groups—and when the speaker (me) is willing to open up about fears and longings, it opens the door for others to do the same.

Suddenly, it becomes personal and intimate as everyone shares what it's like to be human. And for you as the interviewer, you not only test your interviewee's EQ but you get them thinking on the same level on which you hope to talk. As you ask them to identify their feelings and why they had them, you can see their self-knowledge grow before your eyes.

You can see the revelations they have as to why yesterday may have been crappy, wonderful, or both! And if you take it up to current events, you may give them a chance to admit to being nervous for the interview, which gives you a chance to address that nervousness. Which leads me to preparing the setting…

The 5000 Days Project, Seumas (Scotland)

LESSON SEVEN: PREPARING FOR THE INTERVIEW—THE SETTING

The setting is a vital part of the secret sauce. Whether you are working virtually or in person and with or without a camera, the following applies:

PERSONAL COMFORT

Because I film my interviews, adequate light, minimal background audio, external sounds, and comfortable seats are essential. And in the next lesson, we will look in more detail at the physical and technical setting. But one other thing is vital.

I recall once a child who arrived looking tense and afraid. I did my best to assure her that the interview would be fun and that she simply needed to be herself, but she looked more and more miserable as the interview proceeded. Feeling like I was failing her I suggested we take a break. She suddenly looked grateful and said, "Thank you, because I really need to pee."

She then came back relieved and poured her heart out. First and foremost, *make sure that physical needs are met* and that you and your interviewee are comfortable. If the interview is in person, it does not hurt to have a snack standing by should either of you need it.

PRIVACY AND CONFIDENTIALITY

Beyond physical comfort you want to provide emotional comfort and the ultimate key to this

The 5000 Days Project, Dane (Canada)

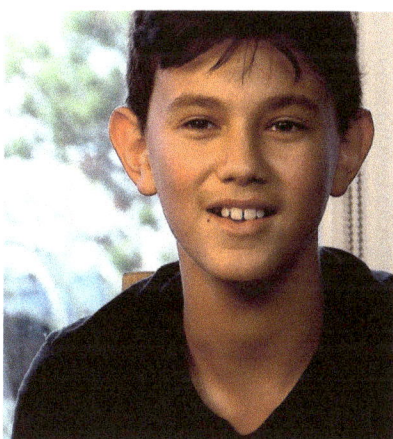

"When any interviewee is guaranteed privacy, they feel much freer to speak their truth."

Dr. Rick Stevenson

is *privacy*. You want to be in a place where your interviewee feels completely comfortable to speak their truth.

If you are interviewing children, due to child safety measures, some schools have arranged rooms with interior windows. Even though everyone is protected if everything is filmed, such a "fishbowl" setting does not have to be embarrassing to the child. You just have to make sure their backs are to the window so that they're not distracted by any potential audience and that their facial expressions are protected.

It is also vital to assure them as to your privacy policy. With all of my 5000 Days Project films, this is the guarantee I give them: "Everything you say to me is private. Your parents have signed off on that guarantee. The only reason that might change is if I think your or someone else's safety might be threatened. Then I will let you know and we'll make a plan together."

Whether you are interviewing kids or adults, when any interviewee is guaranteed privacy, they feel much freer to speak their truth and it dramatically increases the chance the interview will help them.

Confidentiality allows them to go to depths of discussion they might have never had before. Of course, this puts a lot of responsibility in

The 5000 Days Project, Eilidh (Australia)

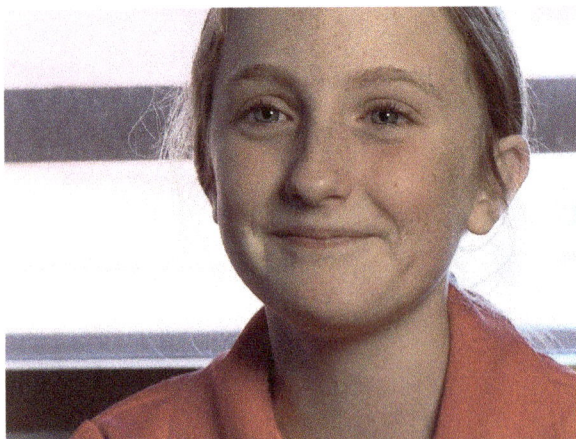

your hands to make the right call. Your intuition is normally the best guide.

In the case of children, if they are holding something back from their parents or a responsible person in their support network, you will want to explore with them why they don't want to share a feeling, fear, concern, or any particular piece of information. As with adults, in the majority of cases you will encourage them to share those things with the right people. If the situation is serious enough, if they are a minor, you will have to make whatever decision is right for them whether they agree or not. See the section on Protocol for Reporting in Lesson Fourteen.

SETTING EXPECTATIONS

Auditions for Children and Teens: From the beginning, I set up all of my potential longitudinal interviews with children and

> "I want people who are open, honest, and tell me the truth, not just what they think I may want to hear."

teens as an audition for one simple reason: I want the young interviewee to want to do it so that there are no victims. If they have to try for it, they become empowered and the whole experience becomes more effective. I tell them I want people who are open, honest, and tell me the truth, not just what they think I may want to hear. I also tell them that they cannot go wrong by simply being themselves. That is what I'm after. Because I have found this process to be effective with most kids, nine out of ten times the audition is actually just the first interview and should be treated the same

The 5000 Days Project, Joey (Australia)

as the others.

Finally, I tell them that it is actually a mutual audition—that they need to check me out, too. It is essential that they are comfortable doing it.

There have been a few cases where I have been unable to get the child comfortable enough to open up, and a few more cases where the child was simply not articulate enough to warrant the money and time. If you feel during the audition interview that the candidate is not yet ready for the process, then it's best to cut the interview short, speak to the parents, and hold off a year. Most of the time, though, the process empowers both parties into a win/win situation and the relationship grows significantly with each passing year.

Let me tell you about a seven-year-old who simply started crying the second I started asking personal questions. While you never wish big negative emotions on anyone, I have often seen that they will be the necessary gate to real progress and revelation. So I tenderly encouraged him but he just kept crying. Suddenly I became worried that perhaps something more serious was going on so I tested those waters but I could find nothing to be concerned about. Still, he just kept crying. Feeling like I was not only failing him miserably but also putting him in pain, I got him a juice and told him that we'd take a break. Luckily, I had immediate access to his school counselor and his parents on the phone and told them about his reaction. Both said that that was his typical reaction when anyone asked him about his feelings, but that he could go home for the rest of the day. I told his parents that I wasn't sure he was ready for the project and they begged me to keep him on, saying that he'd come around. So I did... and he did. And now he's graduating and expresses

The 5000 Days Project, Alice (Zambia)

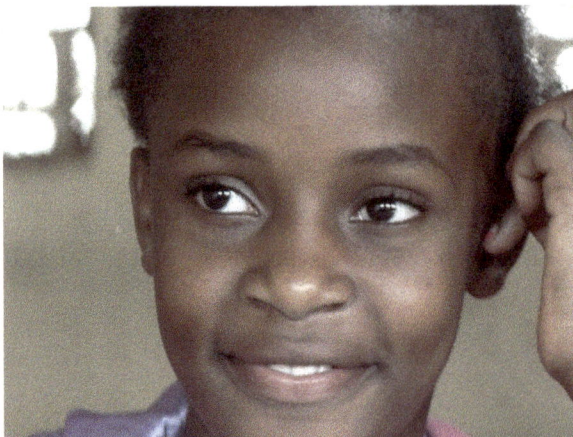

"Adults will say something akin to *I hope I don't cry* in an off-hand way, but one that nonetheless reveals that fear."

himself well. I'm glad that, as a team, we allowed this boy the space he needed to grow.

For Adults: The situation is different for adults. If they are sitting in front of you, they have already decided to participate. However, that is not to say they are without concerns that may need to be addressed. The main concerns are typically two-fold. First, adults need to be assured that everything they are saying is confidential and that the material will be handled and stored with that end in mind. Since they won't be dealing with the material directly, that means they need to be convinced that they can trust you to share the same level of concern. As a Personal Story Mentor, you need to fully honor this concern.

Second, they might be concerned about the emotional places the interview will likely take them. So many adults will say something akin to "I hope I don't cry" in an off-hand way, but one that nonetheless reveals that fear. Having seen tears miraculously spotlight the issue that most needs to be addressed, I personally hope they do… if they need to do so. Tears often open the door to revelation and healing.

Of course, the fact is that none of us like to cry. Crying makes us feel weak and even ugly. It makes us feel cowardly and out of control. Add the old expectation that "boys don't cry" and

Adult-focused "Taking Stock" interviews

Craig Weatherup
Former CEO, Pepsi Co.

The Honorable Mary Bush
Presidential Appointee (IMF); Director of Corporate Boards

you have a cultural burden that, while long out of date, is still a heavy lift. At this point I let them know that being willing to go places that may result in tears is a sign of strength not weakness, courage not cowardice. I may leave it at that or I may talk about how crying is the emotional equivalent of perspiration: it cools us down and it expels toxins. It's a sign of health.

Subtextually, I think they are also asking for permission to cry if the tears emerge. As with kids, if you don't betray a discomfort with it but, in fact, speak about it in a scientific yet empathetic way, you will be giving that permission and creating that safe zone. In fact, I cannot tell you the number of times I have personally spilled tears along with my interviewees. Psychologists might need to remain detached but, as a Personal Story Mentor, you should feel free to honor their tears with your own if you so desire.

CHEAT SHEET

Prep for Children: When preparing for the interview with children, it is helpful to get a parent's perspective. I always ask for their insights into the young interviewee's "dreams, ambitions, struggles, and fears." Most parents who care enough to put the child in something like Personal Story Mentoring give some helpful insights. Some do not—but the exercise helps put the parent in the proper mindset for future follow-up discussions with their kids and includes them in a process that otherwise might exclude them. You want to respect the fact that parents have signed off on trusting their child's secrets with you. That is a lot of trust, so being a communicative partner in the venture is essential.

Prep for Adults: When interviewing adults, the preparation is somewhat different in that you are asking them to provide information and, in

— The 5000 Days Project, Kai Yee (Canada)

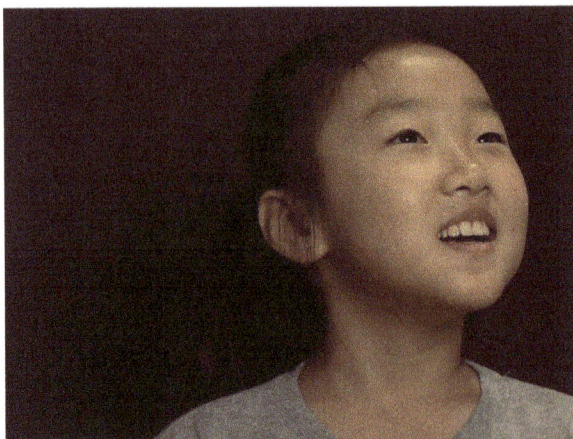

36

some cases, perspective on *themselves*. Hence, it's appropriate to ask for whatever background (bio, resume, etc.) that they think might be helpful. What they give you will say something about what they are comfortable covering. That does not mean you don't go to those other places.

The 5000 Days Project, Sacha (England) / Esme (Scotland) / Pha Kin (Cambodia)

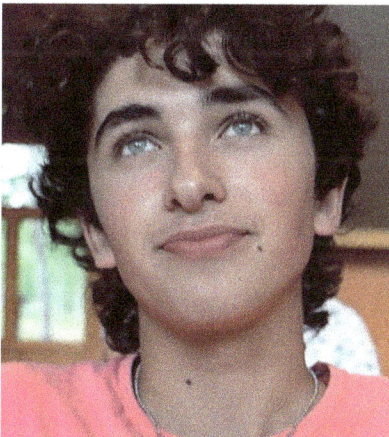

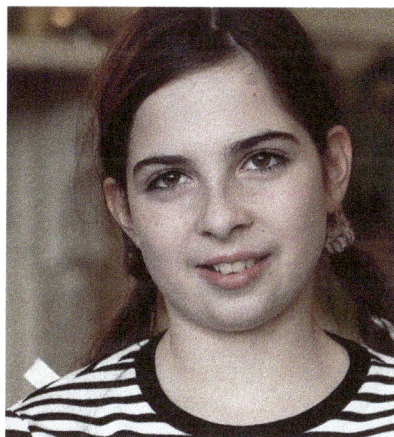

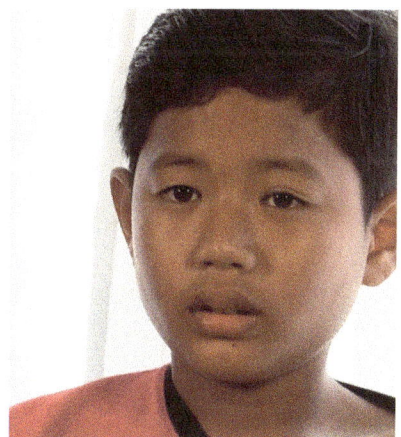

The 5000 Days Project, Chloe (Canada) / Diego (Mexico) / Angela (China)

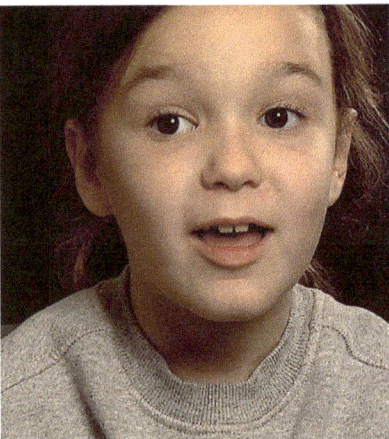

Filming: While the actual interview is all-important unto itself, whether filmed or not, capturing the interview for future use is an important part of the reflection process. Because you are multitasking—listening, processing, offering sage observations and advice while also capturing the interview for posterity—it is important to accept that you will seldom get it all entirely right. So it's important to understand what is most important. Let me explain.

Competing Realities: If you are using a camera, you are responsible for lighting, framing, focus, background, sound, etc., whether you are filming in person or online. When a restless child moves around in a chair —constantly changing your focus—or you have dogs barking or phones ringing, it gets complicated. Add all of that to making your interviewee comfortable and safe while asking the right questions in the right order in the right way, and the challenges multiply. And when certain revelations occur that lead you down new rabbit holes in search of the truth, you are suddenly like the plate-spinner at the circus.

The truth is, you will face this mix of competing priorities in most interviews despite your best preparations. In that case you need to ask yourself what is most important here. Well, that's simple. *It's the interviewee's emotional well-being.* So, if you're in the

— The 5000 Days Project, Mateo (Canada)

Watch excerpts of a young Mateo, who can't sit still, using this QR code.

tinyurl.com/storyq08

> ## "We often lie to ourselves and lie to each other—but facial expressions and body language will reveal the truth."

Dr. Rick Stevenson

middle of a hugely emotional revelation and your camera breaks down, sometimes you just have to accept your technical fate and care for the person. You can't ask them to stop having the experience they're having while you fix the camera. However, if you aren't in the middle of something like that, then you can ask them for a moment while you address the technical needs. In order to get the best interview where the interviewee grows and you can capture

that growth in beautiful HD, you need to have a set of priorities in your head.

They might go as follows:

Emotional state of the interviewee: With or without technical difficulties, the process here *is* more important than the product. And if you're doing your job, you are going to capture loads of beautiful material over several years anyway.

Sound: Authentic dialogue is essential. You can always put B-roll (pictures from their life) over an interview if the picture is out of focus or badly lit but you cannot recreate the authentic sound. That said…

Picture: On the flip-side, *85% of human communication is non-verbal,* so often the picture is worth that thousand words. I've had kids insist they are happy while tears of stress

— The 5000 Days Project in South Africa, and Dyton (Zambia)

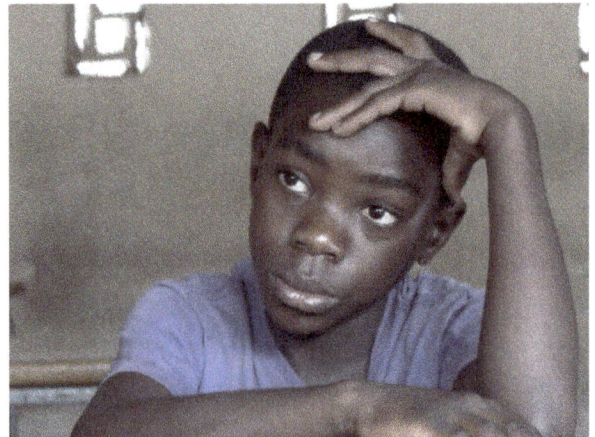

are pouring down their cheeks. We often lie to ourselves and lie to each other—but our expressions and body language will tell us the truth. Beyond this, however, if something is badly lit and the color is off, you can often perform some magic in post-production. That's where the common line "we can fix it in post" comes from!

Light: Seldom do you shoot in a studio where you have control over the light. Here is a perfect example of conflicting priorities. From a camera standpoint, you'd want to shoot in a studio. However, interviewees will feel more comfortable and be more forthcoming if they're in a less formal setting—such as their own rooms. But in a less formal, more natural setting, you will have changing light conditions depending upon the time of day. In that case, you just need to keep your eye on it and if the emotional flow of the interview allows it, fix it.

> "If the story is compelling and good enough, the background will go unnoticed."

Background: Some people like a clean screen background, as it looks more professional. While this is a valid point of view, sometimes you've gone to someone's house and the best natural light is in the laundry room! While you want to avoid too much distraction, I have a theory. It comes from the experience of watching *America's Funniest Home Videos* as a kid. If the story is compelling and good enough, the background will go unnoticed. (If

The 5000 Days Project, Cici (England)

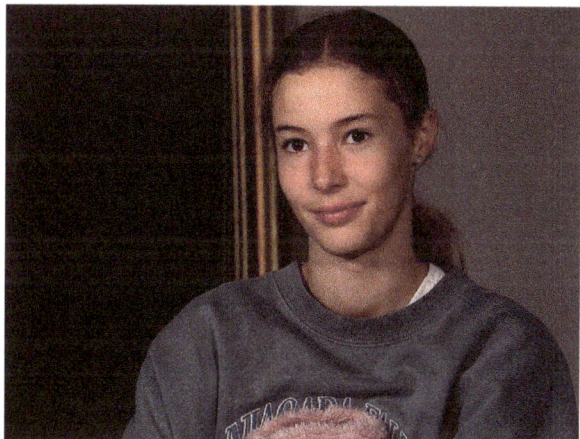

> ## "Loosening up the interview with humor —often the more absurd the better— drops guards and reveals fun selves."

Dr. Rick Stevenson

and when this footage is viewed and audiences are bothered by your background, you've got bigger problems.) Other conflicting priorities will arise and you'll have to make the call. It's natural to feel bad about failing to get the best thing possible but you are the plate-spinner and all of us will fail. I did half of an interview in Mexico once with the camera not even rolling. I've lost footage before and had buzzing microphones. If you get in the habit of glancing at your controls and listening to the sound you're collecting, you will minimize your mistakes and limit them to just a few minutes. But remember, your interviewee's emotional state comes first. Always.

Online Interviews: When doing virtual interviews, you are relieved of much of the burden above... but you still want the picture and sound to be as good as possible. Accordingly, help your interviewee help you help them look good. Send them the link below so that they will be able to prepare as much as possible on their own. Then you can help them fine-tune.

See Appendix A for more details.

SMALL-TALK LEADS TO BIG TALK

Okay. The warm-up! If you are using a camera in-person, you often need some time with the interviewee in the chair in order to focus and

— The 5000 Days Project, Owen (Canada)

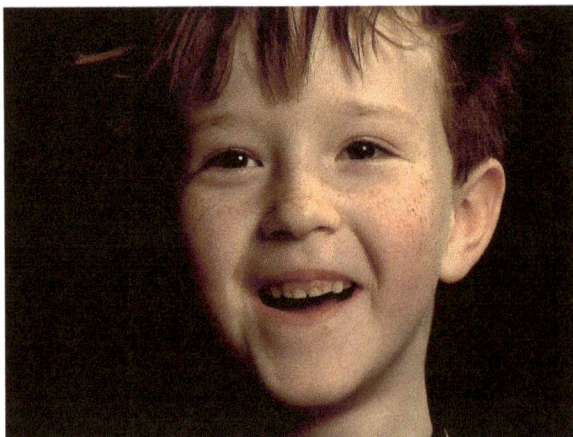

Help your subjects prep for online interviews using the link to this video.

tinyurl.com/storyq09

make sure the light and sound is perfect. Remember, the interviewee may come in nervous, made more so by the presence of the camera, lights, and microphone. If you enter an interview nervous, uncomfortable, or distracted, that will immediately send a message to your interviewee that there is something to be uncomfortable about.

That said, if you start your interview with fun, ease, and natural banter, that will also put them at ease. I have found that loosening them up with humor—often the more absurd the better—allows them to drop their guard and reveal their fun selves.

Eye Contact: During the interview, do your best to never let your eyes leave those of your interviewee. Yes, you may occasionally have to glance at some notes or write something down but the less you do that, the more they forget other distractions—including the fact they are being filmed. The camera itself can be intimidating and, in most cases, the tighter the eye-line (meaning the closer the camera is to the interviewer's face—*your* face), the more personal the footage. Despite that, if you never let your eyes leave the interviewee and ask the right questions, they will forget about the camera very quickly. Same rules apply to online interviews (see technical reference guide for online and in-person interviews). Try to adjust the picture box, moving their face in the frame as close to your own camera as possible.

And, oh yes… remember to press RECORD.

Okay, now… let's talk about the questions!

The 5000 Days Project, Natasha (Canada)

Watch this clip of Natasha loosening up with the use of humor.

tinyurl.com/storyq10

Obviously, the value and efficacy of any interview lies in the quality, specificity, ordering, and delivery of the questions—the "Special Sauce." Everything in this process is aimed at eventually deep-diving into the rabbit holes that the questions will expose. In fact, all of the questions are designed for that specific purpose—opening up rabbit holes so that the individual discovers burrows of revelations.

Hence, the StoryQ Method is definitely more of an art to be interpreted than a science to be applied. What I share here is the result of 7000 personal interviews, over 500,000 clips collected on our virtual technology, endless consultations with talented professionals, and countless successful applications. That said, learn the basics and then see what works.

The basics start with two questions that, when successfully answered, help your interviewees discover 75% of themselves in one fell swoop. The answers to these two questions will likely motivate nearly everything they do—or don't do. The two questions are:

1. What do you really want in life?
2. What are you most afraid of?

In other words, what are your longings and your fears? You are likely driven by your longings and held back by your fears.

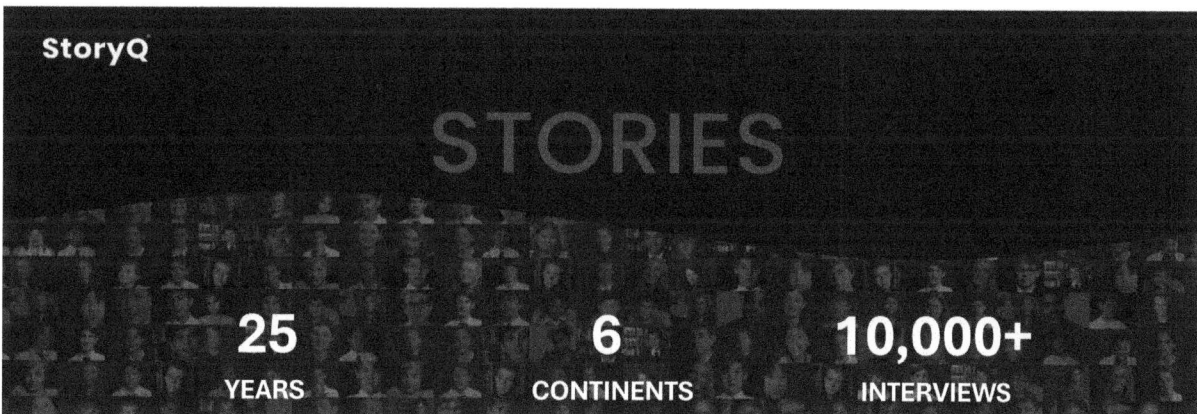

StoryQ

STORIES

25 YEARS

6 CONTINENTS

10,000+ INTERVIEWS

So I want you to ask yourself those questions right now. What do I really want in life? What is my longing?

Here are some typical answers: To fulfill my potential. To leave my mark. To find perfect love. To be known for who I am and be loved anyway. To be rich. To be famous. To be safe and secure. To simply be a good person. To be the best husband or best father. To be happy. To know my purpose.

Personally, my longing has always been related to my purpose. As Mark Twain said, "The two most important days of our lives are the day we are born and the day we discover why."

When 9/11 transformed the 5000 Days Project, I discovered my purpose or greatest longing. I just want to make a difference in the world.

"Your longing provides your narrative drive—and your fear provides obstacles to getting what you really want."

So what do you *really* want?

Now ask yourself the flip side of that. What am I most afraid of? And to get you started, here are some typical fears:

Not being good enough. Disappointing someone. Being ignored, unheard, or neglected. Being uninteresting. Trusting someone. Being betrayed or abandoned. Being alone. Intimacy. Risk-taking. Failure. Success. Being my true self.

— *Mark Twain*

My own fear is obvious to me. Especially at my age. My fear is that I'm running out of time. I want more than anything to make a significant difference, and I fear I won't have enough time to fully accomplish that.

So longings and fears are the key to everything. Your longing provides your narrative drive—and your fear provides the obstacles to you getting what you really want.

One last thing before we detail the questions to open up these doors.

By way of my interviews, I have seen that we all live on a continuum between our longings and our fears.

Where are you on the graph? Where you live on that continuum determines your worldview. Do you see the world as a dangerous place or one filled with potential and hope? Do you see things in abundance or deficit? Are you an optimist or a pessimist? Glass half full or half empty? Take a moment and figure out where you are.

Now, identifying this position with your interviewee will help you understand their mindset. Again, mindset is just the unique human ability to look at exactly the same thing in at least two different ways. For instance, you can be disappointed that a rose bush has thorns or grateful that a thorny bush has roses. It's the same bush.

Remember looking at those Rorschach ink drawings where you can see any number of different things in the same drawing? My favorite illustration of visual trickery to gain perspective is the picture where you either see the duck or the bunny.

People with a darker outlook often see the

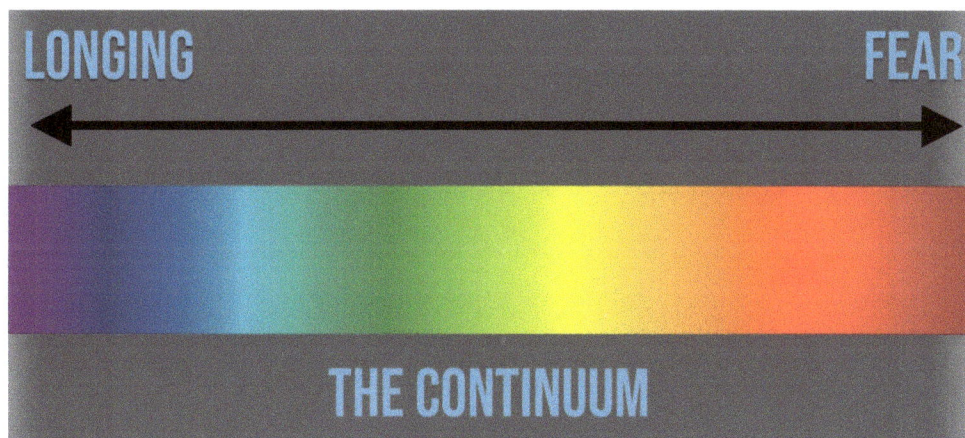

LONGING   FEAR

THE CONTINUUM

duck, oddly enough. When I raise this with kids I ask what changes when they can see two different things in the same picture. Eventually, they realize absolutely nothing changes. It's still the same picture. The only difference is in your outlook. Kids then realize that the way they look at things is strictly a choice. If we can only ever hold 40 thoughts in our heads at the same time, shouldn't we choose those 40 things to work for our better health? My mantra: *Look for the bunny.*

We each own nothing more valuable than our own story. Detailing our story gives us power over it. We become the master of our issues instead of the casualty. Passing this knowledge on to our interviewees is the key to empowering their change and transformation.

Dr. Rick Stevenson

"When you can see two different things in the same picture, absolutely nothing changes. The only difference is in your outlook."

Uncredited illustration from an 1892 issue of Fliegende Blätter

So what are the questions that help us get to the thing the interviewee most needs to discuss? Those questions themselves differ with various ages, as well as the purpose for asking the questions. In Appendices B and C, you will find the loose script I use with each age group to achieve each objective. But before flipping ahead to browse those questions, first review the StoryQ Methodology at our website. It addresses how the process unfolds from introspection to verbalization to revelation to integration. The website also hosts an exceptional video that describes the questioning framework and how our experiences, drivers, and projections are influenced by two potentially competing forces —our emotions and our reasoning. Now, as to how this plays out in the interview, let me reveal the categoric thoughts behind the specific questions.

PASSIONS AND GOALS

Almost immediately, we get down to business. For kids this is, "What do you want to do when you grow up?" or for adults, "Are you currently doing what you ultimately want to do?" Some know, some don't; both replies are revealing, and both get them thinking about dreams, ambitions, and expectations. If interviewees intuitively or overtly know what they want to do, saying so aloud serves as reaffirmation. If they don't have a clue, I encourage them to remove all obstacles and let

StoryQ®

Take time to fully review the StoryQ Method at our website.

tinyurl.com/storyq04

themselves dream the ultimate dream job. A professional billionaire, a movie star, power forward for Barcelona, President of the World... If they can't answer either question, if they can't identify any passion in themselves, then that exposes something deeper that needs to be explored.

PERSPECTIVE

The next series of questions is all about perspective. What has been the best and worst things about the past year? What lessons have they learned about themselves and the world?

These encourage interviewees to get off their road-level view—even out of their foxholes *in the road*—and see their current journeys from a birds-eye view.

FAMILY INFLUENCE AND IDENTITY

The next questions are about family. As a lead-in, I typically ask them to describe each member of their families—using just one word. Because we find our initial identity in our family, each answer is revealing about that identity. For instance, *Mom* descriptors typically range from caring, loving, or nurturing to demanding, bossy, or strict. Sometimes it is distant and descriptive like "drunk" or something reflecting disappointment like "selfish" or "clueless."

Typical *Dad* descriptors range from strong, inspiring, or courageous to undependable, selfish, immature, distant, and absent. Sometimes it is just "no comment" which, in itself, speaks volumes. I will then ask about what the individuals enjoy doing with their parents and what stories they may have—stories that back up their descriptions.

Seeing the road ahead from a bird's-eye view

Watch our short film on perspective, *Connect the Dots*, using this QR code.

tinyurl.com/storyq11

"Articulating that which is your ruler— your measuring stick —is key to eventually becoming *its* ruler."

For siblings, the most popular reply is "annoying," which makes a positive descriptor like "best friend" or "talented" or "supportive" especially unique and revealing.

SELF-IDENTITY

Then comes a big category of questions, including "Describe yourself in one word." This is obviously difficult for most individuals, but also helps them reflect and focus on who they think they really are. Some will say "competitive" or "empathetic" or "ambitious,"

but even a more casual answer like "awesome!" or "confused" is revealing and opens discussion.

The answer is often then the first in what becomes a series of words as I follow up with a request to list their own character strengths. This often requires clarifying that the question is about "who you are" and not "what you do." Some kids have problems with the apparent egocentricity and possible conceit of answering the question, but when they are asked in a matter-of-fact way, most are able to respond. The answers may include enthusiastic, loyal, committed, ambitious, focused, caring, loving, empathetic, good listener, thoughtful, intelligent, funny, generous, and so on. I find it helpful to then ask for a story behind some of the more important descriptors. For instance, "Can you tell me about a time recently when you were 'generous'?" The intention is to get them to tell

as many stories as possible. Stories resonate and land lessons.

Then, on the flip-side, I ask, "And what do you need to work on? What can you do better?" Some individuals have never asked themselves this question before and that in itself is revealing. In such cases, I ask, "So, like Mary Poppins, you are practically perfect in every way?" Then they insist, "No... hold on. Let me think."

For a younger child, you can help them identify something by getting them to recall the comment that is often made by parents directly after that parent yells their name: "Tom, be kinder to your brother," or "Juliette, pick up after yourself!" Most individuals know already, however. The answers will range from "controlling my temper, being kinder, staying focused" to "organization and time management, self-confidence, and being disciplined."

In some cases the same descriptor is used in both strengths and weaknesses—like "being sensitive" or "particular."

The same applies to adults though you may approach it differently. For instance, "What is something you struggle with?"

The answers to questions about strengths are a great launching pad to identify the core of self-worth and identify the tools they possess to help themselves and others.

The answers to questions about the things they need to work on provide a great launching pad to discuss their struggles or burdens. They represent an excellent opportunity for goal setting. Articulating that which is your "ruler"—your measuring stick—is key to eventually becoming *its* ruler.

Earl Stafford, Chairman/CEO
The Stafford Foundation

Charles Meyers, CEO
Equinix

EMOTIONS

The next sequence of questions involves identifying emotions and what elicits them: "What makes you happy? What makes you sad? What makes you anxious or stressed? What makes you jealous? What makes you angry?" Again, encouraging storytelling immediately deepens the understanding behind such emotions. For instance, "I am happiest when I'm playing music. When I'm feeling stressed, if I just pick up my guitar I feel better immediately."

Almost every answer is revealing. If someone says "Video games make me happy," the comment can reveal anything from simply enjoying a simple escape or diversion to the avoidance of reality and pain altogether. If someone says, "I am happiest when I am helping others," that says a lot about their values and what fulfills them. However, if someone says "I'm happiest when other people are happy," that reveals unhealthy or blurred boundaries under the guise of caring about others.

THE MAIN EVENT

The next area is the most sensitive and requires the most care. I ask, "What is the most difficult thing you have ever experienced?" Younger kids don't like to hold on to negative emotions, so even a simple follow-up question like, "When is the last time someone said something mean to you, or something that made you feel bad?" may not yield an answer. However, by age seven to nine, the question starts becoming a powerful revelation because all of us carry some form of childhood trauma, whether it be simple embarrassment or a more severe occurrence like abuse or a tragic accident. This is often the thing they most need to discuss or put in

The 5000 Days Project, Frankie (Canada): Journey of Emotions

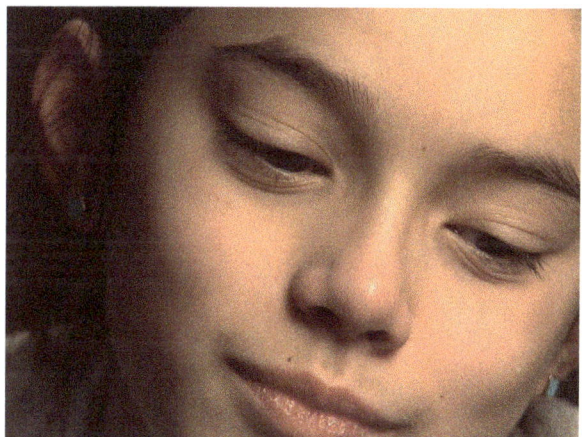

perspective. Obviously, more traumatic inst-ances as they are revealed provide an excellent opportunity to connect the individual with professional help before the situation results in something potentially harmful.

FEARS

The next questions revolve around answering one of the Big Two questions as discussed above—*What are your fears?* Yes, most kids say, "Spiders." However, when I clarify that I'm asking less about visceral fears and more about grander emotional fears, they become more thoughtful. Of course, describing fears of abandonment, neglect, intimacy, failure, or embarrassment is beyond the understanding of most five-year-olds. However, asking them about any "bad dreams" will often tell the story, whether it be monsters in their closet or losing a parent.

"All of our stories in movies and literature are about overcoming our greatest fears. Real life is no different."

For most individuals eight years old and up, the ability to identify their fears is a direct reflection of their level of emotional intelligence. For instance, the child who has lost a parent for whatever reason is often keenly focused on the remaining parent. When we adopted my youngest daughter, Leah, who had experienced neglect thanks to her single-mother's battle with alcohol, Leah had to know where my wife Julie was in the house at all times. Years of hard work went into helping her rewire that part of her brain.

— The 5000 Days Project, Luciano (Chile)

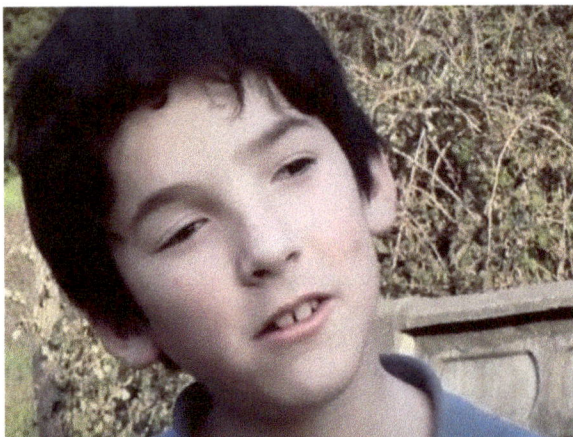

Dr. Rick Stevenson

"If we don't know where we need to go, how are we going to get there?"

Recently, I interviewed a 24-year-old with whom I had started at age five. He had been a quirky, soccer-playing, happy-go-lucky kid up until age fourteen, when his mother packed up and left. Thankfully, his father stepped up and did double duty, as did a number of neighbors and friends. However, during his freshman year at college, his very best friend ended up hanging himself on the goal post of his middle-school soccer field. Once again, someone key in his life "left" him. This set him back and affected his ability to trust relationships until he fully identified and exorcized his fear.

Helping individuals identify their chief fears is the first step in conquering them. All of our stories in movies and literature are about overcoming our greatest fears. Real life is no different. When kids can identify fears, they can gain perspective on their story arc and discover where they need to go. Again, if we don't know where we need to go, how are we going to get there?

LONGINGS

Next, I give them three wishes, which gets to the core of their longings—the second of the Big Two questions. I tell them that they can wish for anything at all except for more wishes. Some cleverly ask for a genie or box that grants requests. I shut that down. They need to prioritize three things.

The 5000 Days Project, Milo (Hong Kong)

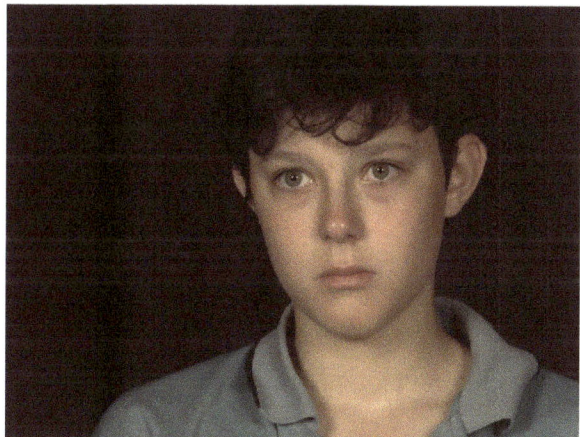

Wishes in the past have run from the social...

- World peace
- End to global warming
- No one goes hungry or without shelter
- My friend's parents get back together
- Our team wins the championship
- That no one would ever be sad

...to the personal:

- No one in my family ever gets sick or dies
- Unlimited money
- That fairies were real
- That I could fly
- I had a dog
- I get to go to Heaven (but not quite yet)

The younger the kid, the more specific the wish. Alternatively, I may have a 4th-grade girl in the U.S. who wants to be president, while a 17-year-old orphan in Cambodia might wish simply for a bicycle, job, and place to live. Some kids might have difficulties coming up with even one wish. These often are the same kids who could not identify their ideal future job or even a passion. This betrays either a fear of dreaming or a fear of making a bad decision. Or a disconnection with their feelings.

All is revealing.

IDEAL FUTURES

I often follow this up with a question about their ideal future. If they could simply write their future, at age 35, what would they be doing? Where would they be living? Would they be in a relationship and/or have children? I stress again before they answer that they are only limited by their imagination. What follows is usually an important reveal about how much they dare to dream.

The 5000 Days Project, Thilo (Germany)

"Rating happiness often reveals the main thing to focus on in the coming year."

ROMANCE

I then ask if they are in love, have a crush, or are in a relationship. No question makes them feel quite as vulnerable as this one, and I can read a lie in their eyes as easily as the large letters on an eye chart. Some individuals absolutely hate the question while others grow to be comfortable with it over time and address it with enthusiasm. I often follow up with a question about whether in the future they plan to get married and possibly have kids. If the answer to kids is yes I ask, "How many?" Ninety percent of the time, the number of kids they choose is exactly the same number of kids that are in their own family.

HAPPINESS

I give them a chance to gauge their level of happiness by rating themselves on a scale of 1-10 with 10 being the happiest. I then ask if they could snap their fingers and change one thing to make that number go up, what it would be. That often reveals the main thing they need to focus on in the coming year. It opens up a chance to verbalize a goal. Recently, one kid said, "I would be much happier if I had a better relationship with my stepmother." Accordingly we explored the potential obstacles, including his stepmother's perceived fears, and plotted a course that would open up dialogue and actions to ameliorate them. He walked away with a measurable goal that might improve his life—and hers.

The 5000 Days Project, Koko (Australia)

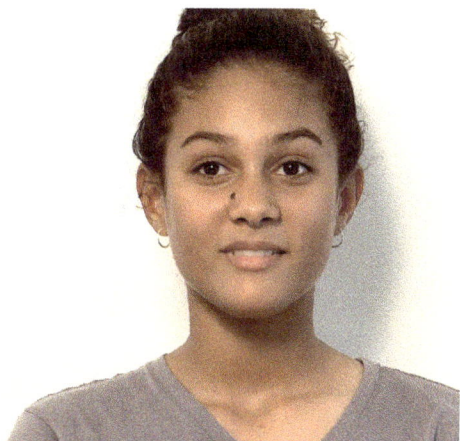

GOAL-SETTING

Here is the perfect chance to have kids establish a goal for the coming year. That goal often emerges directly out of the happiness question.

FAITH

I will often ask a neutral spiritual question like, "If you woke up tomorrow morning and the Creator of the Universe was sitting on your bed, offering you the opportunity to ask one question, any question, what would you ask?" Answers range from "How did it all begin—the origins of the Universe?" to "What is tomorrow's winning lottery number?" This works for kids across the spectrum from budding atheists to those who hold a faith. It allows them to talk about it.

I may even throw in a question helping them identify what they treasure. For instance, "If your house caught on fire and you could only grab one thing, what would it be?" The best answer to this question was given by a 7-year-old who said, "A fire extinguisher?"

IN CLOSING

There are, of course, many more possible questions in the StoryQ Method but those mentioned above are the most essential ones. I usually end with a question about gratitude in hopes of sending them off in a positive state of mind. One such question is, "What are you most grateful for?"

FOLLOW-UP

Finally, I ask them how the interview experience was for them while it is still fresh in their heads. As I've mentioned, there are cases where kids go away in tears. But that's

— The 5000 Days Project, Jacob (Canada)

Dr. Rick Stevenson

normally because they needed some sort of release. However, even in the face of such "trauma," the overwhelming majority of the responses I receive are positive. As one nine-year-old girl said, "It's like a spa for the brain."

"It's like a spa for the brain."

The 5000 Days Project, siblings Nick & Clive (Canada)

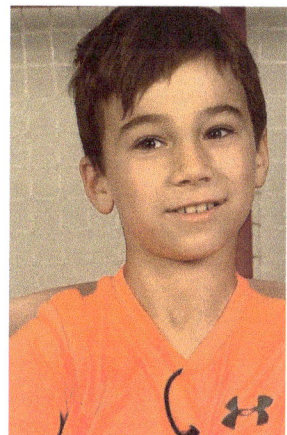

Every movie has a main character, and every main character has a "story arc." The arc is how the main character changes from beginning to end—the central struggle, the issue our main character *must* address in order to solve their problem and become a new version of themselves. It is the change we will cheer for as an audience and is often the change the main character wishes to avoid the most—because it scares them.

In *The Wizard of Oz*, Dorothy thinks that the solution to all of her problems lies "somewhere over the rainbow." By the end of the movie she discovers that she has always held the solution to her problems right where she is, and that there is "no place like home." Jean Valjean in *Les Miserables* is a bitter ex-con who must not only learn to accept grace but also learn to give it. George Bailey in *It's A Wonderful Life* suffers a financial crisis and feels like his life is a failure. In the end, he comes to realize that he's made a huge difference in his world and that that difference is measured not in money but in the quantity and quality of his friends.

Similarly, all of us have at least one arc at any given time. It can be as small as being afraid to try a rope swing, with the arc being finding the confidence to do so. It can be as large as never feeling like we are good enough, and spending a lifetime accomplishing incredible things externally only to finally realize that our cup can only be filled from within.

The Wizard of Oz *and* It's a Wonderful Life

> # "Like in time-lapse photography, you can literally witness your interviewee grow wings."

Dr. Rick Stevenson

Identifying your arc and envisioning its ideal conclusion—what I call the pot of gold at the end of the rainbow—can be life changing. Identifying your arc allows you to name the struggle and start to gain power over it. It provides your blueprint and the structure for a screenplay starring, well, *you*. Identifying the ideal conclusion—the pot of gold at the end of the rainbow—allows you to see your intended destination. After all, how are you going to get to where you need to go if you don't know where THAT is? Once you identify the pot of gold, you can reverse engineer to where you are now… and you've just created the structural framework for your story of transformation.

The arc is likely to be the result of the confluence between your longings and your fears. It will be based on your chief struggle.

Remember me telling you that my chief longing was to make a difference and my chief fear was not having enough time? Well, it's no wonder that my arc has to do with impatience. I have always been hugely impatient. I hate lines, I hate waiting on the phone. I hate traffic lights. So, I have come up with something that has helped me identify my pot at the end of the rainbow. That's the 5000 Days Project. There is nothing like starting a project that *never* ends to teach you patience. I will die doing this project. I just pity the kid who is

The 5000 Days Project, Djazia (England)

there when it happens. "Uh, Mom, I don't think that guy's moving."

So what's your interviewee's arc? It is bound to be their biggest struggle—the one that plagues them, the one that holds them back. If you're doing longitudinal interviews, year after year, this arc will become apparent and watching them identify it and deal with it is one of the truly satisfying aspects of Personal Story Mentoring. Like in time-lapse photography, you can literally witness your interviewee grow wings.

If you're interviewing someone on film over several years and they request a short film upon reaching 18 or 22 (post-college), the arc you identify in your notes will provide the backbone of their story. Track their longings, fears, and growing arc each year so that you can help them map their progress and keep them accountable to their own goals.

Following the interview, you will want to immediately jot down your notes and observations while they are fresh in your mind. If it is a one-off "Taking Stock" interview with an adult, your notes will help the editor capture your point of view on the story. If it is a longitudinal interview, your notes will provide a welcome bit of background a year later when you take them through their next interview. Even though you may only spend an hour or so a year with the interviewee, the reminder allows you to pick up right where you left off and continue to build an intimate Personal Story Mentor relationship. The form included at the end of this lesson is the recommended format.

LESSON TWELVE: AFTER THE INTERVIEW

Along those lines, I also send a follow up note to parents keeping my comments general enough to respect the child's privacy but often with an observation or two. I also take a few minutes to race high speed through the footage and pull out a few wonderful screen grabs that capture the character of the child. You have seen examples of these screen grabs throughout these Lessons—not all of which are sent to parents.

While there are far more talented and experienced photographers than myself, I often get credit for sending pictures that so capture the personality of the child that those pictures end up as the perfect screensavers on their parents' computers for the coming year.

The 5000 Days Project, Georgie (Zambia)

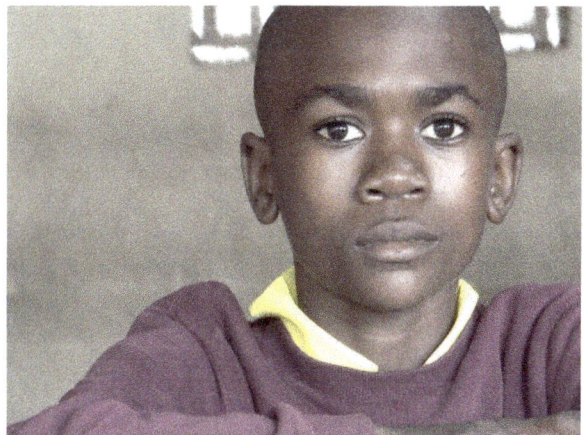

My secret? I have thirty frames per second over a sixty-minute interview—or over 10,000 frames to choose from. While I don't have time to consider all of them, the sheer number of possibilities will almost always guarantee that I come up with something great.

Finally, there is the technical matter of getting the digital footage of the actual interview banked into multiple safe places of storage. Despite the fact that the main value is in the interview itself, it is vital that this is done properly, immediately. I have lost or accidentally erased footage before and it is gut-wrenching because you have lost a piece of history that cannot be recovered.

Dr. Rick Stevenson

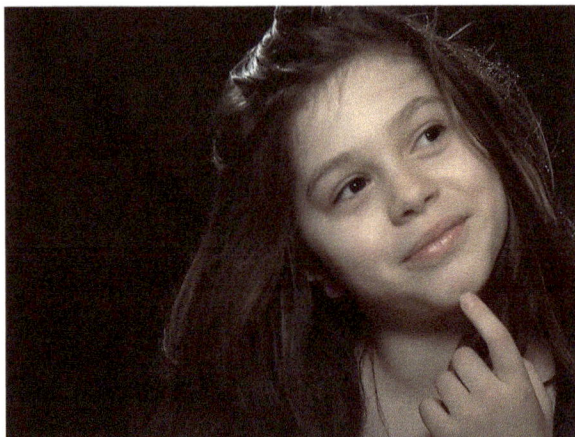

StoryQ

STORYQ / 5000 Days Project
INTERVIEW QUICKSTART CHECKLIST
THE QUESTIONS: QUESTION SET, Ages 4-6

Interviewer/ PSM:

Interview Candidate:

Age:

Parents Name & Contact:

Date of Initial Contact with
Parent or Child:

Interview Date & Time:

Interview Format: In-Person/Film   Zoom-based Online

Interview Location:

Relevant Background Info of
Interviewee:

Referral?

Other Pertinent info:

Video File Name & Size:

Video File Location:

GETTING STARTED Checklist:
o   IF ZOOM based, Confirm CLOUD RECORDING Settings, including Create audio transcript.
     TOPIC: Interviewee Name, Age- 5000Days* _ InterviewerLastName (*or StoryQ/Taking Stock, etc)
o   RECORDING ON?
o   CONFIRM Subjects lighting and audio are optimal, especially as light changes
o   Present PRIVACY GUARANTEE:
     Everything you say or share with me is private, and your parents have signed off on that
guarantee. The only reason that might change is if I think your, or someone else's safety might be
threatened. Then I will let you know and we ll make a plan together. Sounds good?

LESSON THIRTEEN: PSYCHOLOGY AND PERSONAL STORY MENTORING

My life was changed for the better with the help of a trained psychologist. As I have shared before, I was a 37-year-old man who, despite my desire since age seven to find the right person to have a family, had failed time and time again to find the right person.

A couple sessions into my personal therapy, my problem became clear when my therapist had me describe every person I had ever dated. After doing so in glowing terms she asked what the problem was. I replied that I didn't feel absolute certainty about any of them. She then asked what they all had in common, and the answer was too obvious to ignore. It was *me*. I was what they all had in common.

As previously shared, the problem was not with everyone else. The problem was with me. BOOM. This was not the least bit insulting. In fact, it was an absolute relief because I realized that if it was my problem, I could fix it—and that is what I did over the next months. Through Family of Origin therapy—in which you write down every past influence you can remember—I slowly gained perspective on my life. Sure enough, when the right person did come along in the person of my wife Julie, I was able to recognize it.

Upon reflection, the stigma that I had attached to therapy kept me away from it. The fact that I did not have any huge mental health problems kept me away from dealing with the smaller

— Rick Stevenson. BOOM.

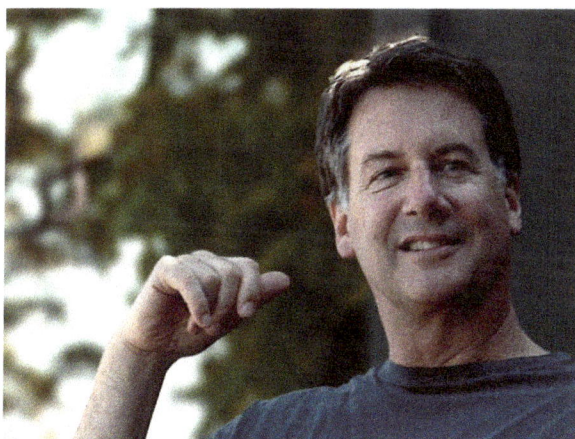

"Most people don't have the skills or the relationships where focused and informed discussion can truly take place."

Dr. Rick Stevenson

ones. When I think about how lucky I was to be "forced" into therapy against my prejudices… when I think how lucky I was to have the money to pay for it… when I think how lucky I was to find right therapist when, as in any field, there are good ones and not so good ones… it seems a blessing of the highest order that I was able to get the help that changed my life. That experience not only changed my life by helping me find the right person but it has led to this field I am in now

—the field that has become my life's purpose.

This is all my way of saying that I have nothing but huge respect and gratitude for the good psychologists out there. That said, the experience also convinced me that while everyone could gain from professional therapy, we have neither the depth in numbers nor the resources to serve everyone in this way. Add this to the stigma that kept me and others away from therapy, and you realize that there has to be a better way.

It led me to realize that the grand majority of the public falls into a lane that is currently not being served. There are people with genuine psychological problems like schizophrenia, bipolarity, narcissism, and so on that can only be treated by the right therapist. Then there are the rest of us who struggle with our own ignorance, who need help but never get that help. We think we can just "talk to our friends"

Rick in therapy

but most people don't have the skills or the relationships where focused and informed discussion can truly take place.

So, what is the solution? As recently as a decade ago, your only option to deal immediately with an injury or a sickness was to go to the emergency room. Remember how these things always occurred on weekends when you could not get in to see your doctor—a doctor who was always booked one month in advance anyway? And then, if you were not visibly dying, you'd often sit in the waiting room for six hours with a horde of other marginally-sick or injured people just to get treated for something that really did not require the resources of the emergency room. Despite this, you were still charged all of the fees. In my case it was almost $5000 for a broken finger— and that was just to put a cast on it until a doctor could take it off and set it. I was lucky enough to find one later that day so the entire episode was a waste of time and money—and had almost nothing to do with good health.

Luckily, in the last several years, we have wisely developed local medical drop-in centers to deal with these things. It has transformed medicine and freed up emergency rooms to deal with emergencies. Now we have neighborhood facilities where we can see trained personnel to deal with myriad problems that fall short of major ones. Are you seeing the analogy to our current mental health crisis?

So, Personal Story Mentoring can be a vital service to the vast majority of the public that does not get served by traditional psychology. In fact, I'll go so far as to say that while some Personal Story Mentors will either be psychologists or have a background in it, others will have backgrounds that serve the cause of mentoring at least as well as a psychologist.

The 5000 Days Project, Zander (Canada)

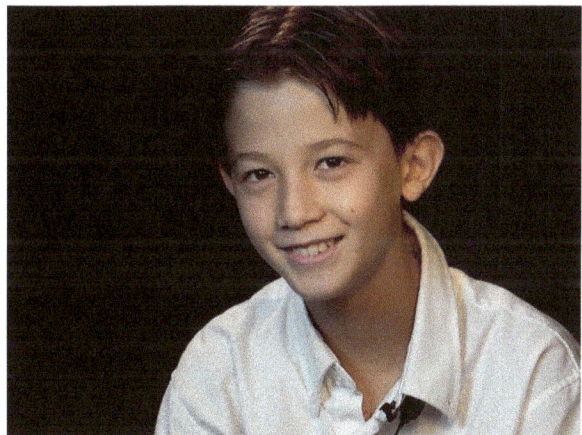

"We tend to live our lives like we're standing in front of a 100-foot painting of ourselves... but we're only one foot away."

Dr. Rick Stevenson

In fact, psychologists are bound by a strict code of conduct that limits the extent to which they can bring themselves to the process. Those guidelines are there for a reason. That said, the advantage of personal mentoring is that you are unapologetically there as their mentor. Yes, you may be there to lend a non-judgmental ear and guide your interviewee with questions that will help them discover themselves and solve their greatest mystery, "Who in the world am I?" But you are also there to get involved, to encourage them. You're there to empathize, share your personal experience, and let them know you have their confidence and their back. When I look back at the role of mentors in my life, I have to credit them with having more positive influence than anything or anyone else. No contest.

A STORY-BASED PROCESS

We tend to live our lives like we're standing in front of a 100-foot painting of ourselves and we're only one foot away. What do we see? A few brush strokes, maybe some errors? Just a small part of the picture. Through Personal Story Mentoring, the StoryQ Method helps our interviewees stand back so that they can see the whole picture and gain perspective. It allows them to connect the dots of their lives. The StoryQ Method is all about asking the right questions, in the right way, in the right order, in the right setting that will help the

Self-discovery is like connecting the dots

interviewee get to their right answers. Beyond asking questions, you are there largely to listen and help them make their own discoveries.

I have seen first hand how the grand majority of us are born with this deep pool of wisdom that, when accessed in the right way, can help us find the way to our right answers. This pool of wisdom is accessed by self-knowledge, and getting there requires the skills of someone who can help us. That could be a psychologist —but not only does the stigma, cost, and lack of accessibility keep us away, there are protocols that psychologists rightly follow that make "mentoring" not an option for them. Yet for those of us who have also been on the receiving end of good mentoring, it may be exactly what we need and, in fact, all we need.

The beauty of StoryQ's Personal Story Mentoring is that almost everyone is comfortable telling a story. While telling their own story can be a challenge, most people who are willing to give it a try become huge fans of the process once they've done it. It's about building Emotional Intelligence, or EQ. As I have written earlier, if knowledge is power, self-knowledge is superpower—and 80% of us can solve our emotional issues if we are introduced to the tools.

Review the StoryQ Methodology at our website using this QR code.

tinyurl.com/storyq04

Conventional wisdom tells us that triggers—those things that send us back into the difficult experience of a traumatic event—are bad. They can be dangerous, yes… but they can also be liberating—a key indicator of a pain that needs addressing. In fact, a lot of cognitive and narrative therapy is based on getting the tormented individual to confront the original event enough times that it begins to lose power over them. It works like vaccines—giving you a small dose that imitates the original virus but in amounts where your body can handle and process it. Eye Movement Desensitization and Reprocessing (EMDR) works in similar ways. In fact, if you remember my story about my nephew Andy in an earlier lesson, it represents this method of telling something enough times that it starts to lose power over us.

All of that said, unless you are a trained psychologist, you'll want to avoid situations beyond your expertise and ideally have someone standing by with that expertise. However, sometimes your line of questioning will unlock something that you have to deal with at the moment. Such was the case with Danielle, who has bravely volunteered her story to help other people in her situation. See below.

As you can see, I did not anticipate "the guy in the black shirt" showing up in the interview. Nor the fact that he had a gun and was

The 5000 Days Project, Danielle (USA)

Watch a portion of Danielle's complete story using this QR code.

tinyurl.com/storyq12

threatening to kill me. What I did know is that he probably represented the side of Danielle that felt shame for the molestation and that he needed to be disempowered. Nonetheless, I did follow up with Danielle's mother who passed on the episode to her psychologist. But talking him down worked. After that day, he never showed up again.

The reason we have a negative opinion of triggers is that they are never welcome. They show up and scare us. And sadly, when it comes to sexual abuse, the problem is far greater than we want to think. The National Sexual Violence Resource Center (NSVRC) reports that 1 in 3 of female rape survivors are aged 11 to 17, and that 20% of all females have been subjected to rape or attempted rape. Sadly, I think the percentage is higher than that. In fact, the ME TOO movement has expanded the public dialogue about sexual violence to include any form of unwanted

Dr. Rick Stevenson

> "Many teachers won't have hard discussions with their students for fear of finding something out that they are required to report to public agencies."

touching. Having heard a number of these stories, the impact is devastating. And it does not just involve girls. We need to do better and talk about it openly. Taking it out of hiding is a vital step in addressing it.

1 in 5 Women Victimized

Learn more at the National Sexual Violence Resource Center website.

tinyurl.com/storyq13

PROTOCOL FOR REPORTING

So, what do we do when confronted with something that might need to be reported?

As private Personal Story Mentors, we are not under the same must-report guidelines as public employees. This is both good and bad. On the good side, I have spoken to many teachers who simply won't have these necessary discussions with their students for fear of the potential of "finding something out" that they need to report. This leaves a lot of kids without the support they might need. On the teacher's part, however, this is not cowardice. Teachers are put in the impossible position of having to report even though the circumstances may be very questionable and there may be false accusations as a result. There have to be guidelines, however, and, as with all guidelines, one size does not fit all.

On the negative side, that means the call is up to us, and that is a scary responsibility. To this end I am always led by two principles which we can consider as our StoryQ Protocol.

1. In general, follow the guidelines of public employees regarding abuse. Guidelines for both mandatory and voluntary (permissive) reporters vary from jurisdiction to jurisdiction. See below for an example from Washington State.

2. When in doubt, ask if this child is in danger or a danger to someone else. If the answer to this is *no*, you can use your discretion. If the answer is *yes* but complicated, bring it to your StoryQ Mentor supervisor for advice. This should provide the wisdom you need to make a good decision.

Review Washington State's guidelines for mandatory and permissive reporting.

tinyurl.com/storyq14

For maximum effectiveness, our goal as interviewers should be to ask the right questions, in the right way, in the right order, in the right setting to help the interviewee get to *their* right answers. This is our primary role because the process of discovery and revelation is at its best when it comes from within.

To that end, before I resort to giving advice, a great technique is to offer up a question that de-personalizes the situation the individual is struggling with and lets them attempt to arrive at their own solution.

For instance, one young teen was struggling with the oppressive weight of needing to impress his peers—the most familiar of teen burdens. He even shared how he had been bullied, which had led him to turn around and bully those "below" him. Five minutes after this statement, I said, "If a friend came to you and was struggling with wanting to impress his friends and sometimes that led him to treat others badly, what advice would you give him?" Without hesitation, he replied, "I'd tell him that treating others badly will make him feel like shit and if he needs to do that to impress this certain group of friends, they are not the friends he needs." As I looked at him, the realization hit him and he hung his head. After a moment he looked up with an ironic smile. "It's pretty simple, isn't it?" I nodded. He had just taken a sip from the deep well of wisdom within him. All he needed was a cup.

The 5000 Days Project, Cristian (Mexico)

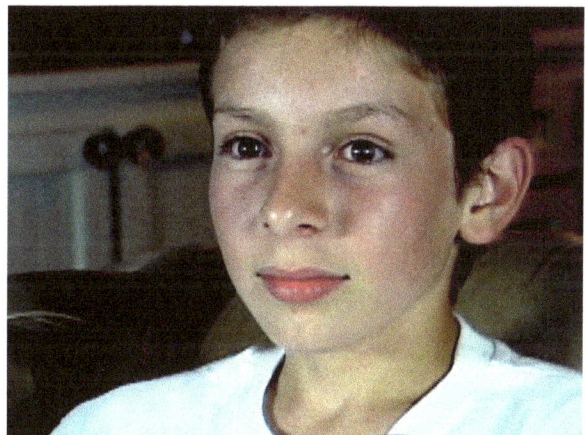

That said, the uniqueness and power of the StoryQ Method—whether you are a Personal Story Mentor for youth or as a facilitator for adults as they "take stock" of their lives—lies in the selective sharing of your own experience. When you choose to share and be vulnerable, it opens the door for the same in return. What you choose to share will vary based on where you are in your own life and whatever wisdom or insight you may have garnered along the way. I've discovered that sharing something personal has a variety of benefits.

First, it can make the interview more of a conversation in spots between two mutually-vulnerable individuals, which helps diminish the stigma of a therapist's couch and the fear of judgment.

Second, personal stories stick where theories and psychological platitudes are lost on most listeners. Just watch an audience when a speaker is speaking. They sit back when lectured and lean in during stories.

Finally, the danger of sharing any stories, thoughts, or theories is that you may be somehow off base and the last thing you want to do is damage. However, if you own your

> "Ask the right questions, in the right way, in the right order, in the right setting to help the interviewee get to *their* right answers."

Dr. Rick Stevenson

own experience and offer it up as just that, the individual can and will decide for themselves if it resonates.

With the knowledge that each interviewer/mentor/facilitator will bring his or her own wisdom to the table, in the next lesson I will offer up the benefit of my own as an extended example. You are, of course, free to take this or leave this, but I'll detail how I may respond to a list of stressors for all people but especially teens. I welcome you, the reader, to add to this pool of wisdom/advice as we all can never truly get enough of it.

The 5000 Days Project, Charlie (Canada)

LESSON SIXTEEN: COMMON TOPICS AND POTENTIAL ANSWERS

Throughout my two decades of interviews, I have identified a number of common topics that keep emerging and I will share them with you on the following pages. These initially emerge in kids and teens but—if they have not been processed and dealt with in a healthy way —they may still be present in adults. This just further goes to support my theory that most of what we still struggle with as adults involves some form of arrested development from our youth—some unfinished business where our maturation process stalled.

I recently interviewed a man in his eighties who simply did not have the vocabulary to talk about his feelings. Sure enough, an influential incident at age ten involving a distant father with similar difficulties seemed to seal this man's emotional access—for life. It is not something that a Personal Story Mentor is likely to change given seventy years of habit, but you can help source their relationship with feelings up to age ten and identify the influential incident that set the course for their future. You can also explore the fear of vulnerability, weakness, disappointment, or whatever it may be that fuels that behavior and the seemingly positive/negative impact it has had on their lives. The point being: it is almost all based in childhood, and if you can find the child within the person at any age, you are likely to unlock some helpful doors.

Granted, most of the adults who sign up for a

Not all of us are equipped or prepared to talk about our feelings

Taking Stock interview are not seeking nor expecting transformational change. They are simply there to capture their personal history on film. That said, half of these interviews turn out to be revelatory providing the interviewee with a refreshing surprise. In that way, these interviews can be like a friendly Trojan Horse —the unexpected gift being transformation. If this occurs, it has likely occurred either because the interviewee is hungry for it or because you have created a safe environment where they can explore their past. This gives you the chance to look for the wormholes connecting their consciousness to their unconscious selves.

At minimum, these interviews provide a new perspective on a previously unexamined life. By verbalizing their story, the individual gains an additional degree of claim over the territory they are often unaware that they actually own.

In conclusion, when it comes to fellow adult interviewees, many of whom may be older than you, your role as a Personal Story Mentor is more nuanced and subtle. If, in the exploration of their past, you can help them discover themselves with new eyes, it is likely to come through observing that which moves them in a specific way and then exploring that area to the extent to which they are willing. Hence, my experience is that most people are hungry for this form of exploration even though it makes them feel deeply vulnerable. As with a senior getting health advice from a doctor in their 30s there may be initial hesitation but ultimately the senior still is after the knowledge the young doctor offers.

Now, the great advantage of working together as Personal Story Mentors is that we can build a bank of experience shared through stories that might just be the answer to someone's greatest struggle. For this reason, I have banked my own experiences on the facing page for starters.

MOST COMMON TOPICS

- NEGATIVE THOUGHTS, SELF-DOUBT

- BODY IMAGE / PHYSICAL APPEARANCE

- FEAR OF JUDGMENT, SELF-CONSCIOUSNESS

- FEELING AT ODDS WITH ONESELF OR DISSOCIATION

- NOT FEELING LIKE YOU ARE GOOD ENOUGH

- COMPETITION; GRADES OR PERFORMANCE REVIEWS: FEAR OF FAILURE

- THE IMPACT OF SOCIAL MEDIA

- RUMOR

- GRIEF, LOSS, AND DEATH

- STRESS ABOUT DEADLINES

- LACK OF MOTIVATION / PRESSURES AT SCHOOL

- SCHOOL / WORK: ATTITUDE VS. GRATITUDE

- FEAR OF NOT BELONGING, LONELINESS

- FAMILY ISSUES

- GLOBAL WARMING, RACISM, HUNGER, POVERTY, INJUSTICE

- FOMO—FEAR OF MISSING OUT

- BULLYING

- SUICIDAL THOUGHTS

- VULNERABILITY, INSECURITY, AND WEAKNESS

- AN UNCERTAIN FUTURE

NEGATIVE THOUGHTS & SELF-DOUBT

I love sharing the following legend. It speaks to the power we have over our mysterious minds.

An old Cherokee was teaching his grandson about life. "A fight is going on inside me," he said to the boy. "It is a terrible fight and it is between two wolves. One is evil—filled with anger, envy, sorrow, regret, greed, arrogance, self-pity, guilt, resentment, inferiority, lies, false pride, superiority, and ego."

He continued, "The other wolf is good—filled with joy, peace, love, hope, serenity, humility, kindness, benevolence, empathy, generosity, truth, compassion, and faith. The same fight is going on inside you—and inside every other person, too."

The grandson thought for a minute and then asked his grandfather, "Which wolf will win?"

The old Cherokee simply replied, "The one you feed."

Once we discover that what we focus on is up to us—*our choice*—we can use the power of mindset to feed the right wolf. Remember, you can be angry about a rosebush for having thorns or you can be grateful for a thorn bush having flowers. Mindset is the unique human ability to look at exactly the same thing two different ways.

BODY IMAGE & PHYSICAL APPEARANCE

For years, I posed this uncomfortable question in my 5000 Days Project interviews: "Take one hundred kids your age. Where among those hundred would you rank yourself in terms of looks, with 100 being the best looking?" In contrast to the other thirty-odd questions—which kids generally enjoyed answering because it was like solving a puzzle for them—

——— Two Wolves *(Franz Marc, 1913)*

Dr. Rick Stevenson

> "Shared ideas of what is beautiful are thrown at us in the media from the moment we can sit up and watch television."

this question was by far their least favorite. They squirmed, saying they didn't know or that they didn't want to seem conceited. I told them not to worry about sounding conceited; this was just a simple question about how they perceived themselves. They eventually, reluctantly, all got around to a number.

By the end of interviews, though, something extraordinary happened. They would become the number they gave. This was the case in spite of what number society might have given them at first glance. Of course, this "you are what you feel you are" phenomenon is not particularly ground-breaking, psychologically. However, seeing the evolution of the process unfold before me was fascinating. A model-ready girl with low self-esteem might say "I'm around 20" and mean it without a shred of false humility. On the flip-side, an average looking boy might say "99!" and grin as wide as the Grand Canyon. And sure enough, their level of self-confidence and self-esteem and degree of egocentricity would bear out the uttered number by the end of the interview. The so-called average looking boy would begin to shine, and the so-called beautiful girl would fade.

Obviously, beauty is subjective; but there are

"The best plastic surgery is confidence." Fashion photography, Ghana-style

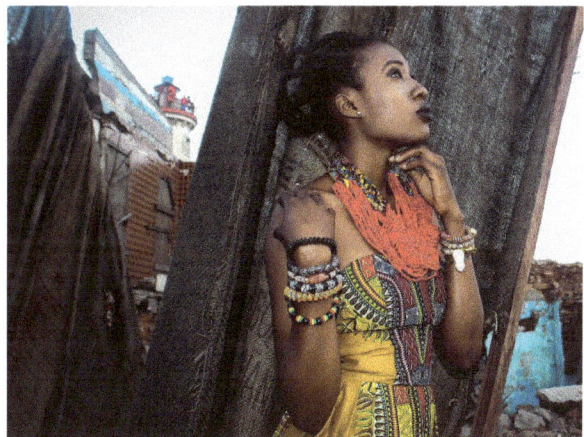

certain features that society seems to agree upon and cause some people to end up with modeling contracts or getting cast in movies. Thanks to the billions of dollars that advertisers spend each year to let us know how badly we each need their products, shared ideas of what is beautiful are thrown at us in the media from the moment we can sit up and watch television. Hence, the question I have asked, as awkward as it may be, is helpful in identifying how much children's self-images have been influenced by such external influences. This is especially true as it relates to body image.

In this way, the best thing you can do as a mentor is let them know that confidence is the best plastic surgeon. Challenge them to think about a friend or classmate who doesn't seem to care—who wears their "imperfections" convincingly. In fact, those imperfections become a part of their character—things that make them unique. We all know friends or even celebrities who have had vanity plastic surgery. More often than not, while that surgery may have lessened a perceived imperfection, the individual loses the character in their face that made them special in the first place. Note Jennifer Grey's career following *Dirty Dancing.* She may have been self-conscious about her nose, but it was decidedly part of her "look."

I've always had a prominent nose which became especially apparent and annoying around puberty. It definitely took a while for my face to catch up. I was also extremely skinny—like "turn sideways and you almost disappear" skinny. These flaws, however, became my best friends because they forced me to develop my character, my intellect, and my other talents—things that would last forever versus things that would fade with age. There are few things sadder than beautiful

Dr. Rick Stevenson

Rick's turn-sideways-and-disappear phase

"Those who worry about what others think of them become their prisoners."

people who have based their stock and self-worth in their looks only to be left with nothing as those looks fade with age. This is especially evident in many adult women. One teen beauty queen, Maureen McCormick ("Marcia Brady" in *The Brady Bunch*), has written a telling memoir which is evidence of this trap. (See the link below.)

FEAR OF JUDGMENT & SELF-CONSCIOUSNESS

If there is a salient teen disease, fear of judgment is it. Because the self is not yet fully formed, we tend to try to see and discover ourselves through the eyes of others. Nine out of ten teens struggle with this problem, and half of those never grow out of it—which means it's an adult disease as well. To paraphrase Lao Tzu, "Those who worry about what others think of them become their prisoners."

When we try to define ourselves through others or through our sports, grades, accomplishments, and so on, we are giving all of our power away and are placing our fragile selves in external places outside of our control. And when we give the power away it is often to people who don't want it. As my father used to say to me when I was a teen and worried about what others thought, "Rick, you would not care so much about what others think about you if you realized how seldom they do." Sure enough, others are wrapped up in their own problems and focused on themselves. However, as they learn that the only source of

—— *Maureen McCormick and Davy Jones on the set of* The Brady Bunch

Read *Entertainment Weekly*'s review of McCormick's book *Here's the Story.*

tinyurl.com/storyq15

"self-worth" is in the name—from one's *self*—they gain a new sense of control because they alone can decide who they want to be. That is why I ask them to describe themselves in one word and then follow up with having them list their character strengths. Some will find this awkward because they think it's being boastful. Assure them that it is not about conceit, it's about self-knowledge. And not to worry, you'll be asking them about their perceived weaknesses as well.

FEELING AT ODDS WITH ONESELF & DISSOCIATION

I would suggest that most of us, most of the time, feel at least a bit out of tune. That's when our actions, thoughts, behavior, and words don't totally coincide with who we really are.

When I was going through therapy with the intention of finding out why I had trouble committing to getting married, my therapist asked me how I handled various situations within my current relationship. Having already gone through Family of Origin therapy sharing everything I knew about my parents, she observed that I was reacting exactly like my dad had reacted in similar situations. She said, "No wonder you have trouble knowing how you truly feel in the relationship when you're being someone else in it." I was seriously out of tune.

I can attest to the fact that during those times you are in tune with your true self, there is nothing better. It's the ultimate form of peace. Again, from the thoughts of Lao Tzu, "If you are depressed, you are living in the past. If you are anxious you are living in the future. If you are at peace, you are living in the present." Just like a lie necessitates a number of additional lies, when you always tell the truth you are relieved from having to keep up false pretenses. If connection is the source of

"The only thing worse than feeling pain is feeling nothing at all."

"The pain we feel is a warning system, a sign that something needs to be addressed."

happiness, connection with oneself is the ultimate source. We all know those rare people who feel 100% comfortable in their own skin. They are so easy to be around. We also all know the well-worn advice, "You might as well be yourself because everyone else is taken."

Dissociation has become a go-to coping mechanism for many—especially teens. It is defined as "a mental process of disconnecting from one's thoughts, feelings, memories, or sense of identity." People tend to dissociate from themselves for a variety of reasons, especially as a means of pain relief. If they don't like—or don't think they can handle—what they're feeling, they check out. It's usually triggered by some stimuli associated with a previous trauma. This is a more extreme example of being out of tune with oneself and leads to numbness, not feeling anything at all. And it's the latter that is a primary cause of cutting among teens. Many of those who become "cutters" have gone numb and cut just to bring some feeling back.

As an interviewer, you can start by observing what people who dissociate come to discover: The only thing worse than feeling pain is feeling nothing at all—and we'll have plenty of time to feel nothing when we're dead. We feel pain for a reason. It's a warning system that something needs to be addressed. Pain coming from a specific trauma may never totally go away, but it can be significantly diminished by taking a deep breath and confronting it verbally. There are some traumas so extreme that only a specialist should shepherd them through the process. But we, ourselves, can deal with most of our pain if we're willing to go there.

Recently, I was asked this question: *"So how do you handle the situation if a teen or younger kid admits to cutting or they disclose that their friend does? How do you proceed in that confidentiality slippery slope besides asking how they have handled it so far, alerting a trusting adult, and so forth?"*

I start each interview reviewing the privacy policy (see Lesson Seven, page 32). As previously stated, the beauty and challenge of being a Personal Story Mentor is that you are not bound by the same requirements for reporting as a teacher or public employee. These re-

quirements are there for a reason but they don't take into account the gray area. If a child is potentially suffering abuse, the requirement to report to the police is a good one but can sometimes result in an even greater danger for the child. Again, I have had the best teachers tell me that for this reason, they "don't want to know" and hence "don't ask." As a Personal Story Mentor, you get to make a judgment call, which may involve a number of other more clever and sensitive ways to solve the problem.

Likewise, if the child knows that telling the truth will automatically result in getting their parents in trouble with the police, they simply won't tell the truth and the problem goes unaddressed. However, if they can trust that you'll handle the situation sensitively, they trust you and share what needs to be shared.

Obviously, it's not a perfect science and I always err on the side of reporting, following

> **"Emerging evidence suggests that verbal journaling may be many times more effective than written journals."**

public employee guidelines most of the time. However, as a Personal Story Mentor, you have the opportunity to solve problems others cannot solve.

You will likely recall the story I told about my nephew Andy in the introduction. The current hole in most SEL (social and emotional learning) curricula is the complete lack of verbal journaling options. We all know of the huge body of evidence surrounding the value of journaling, but the emerging evidence suggests that verbal journaling may be many times more effective.

Remember the amygdala? The brain science behind it is fascinating. All of our emotion comes from this tiny almond-shaped thing in our brain called the amygdala. Anger, fear, love, infatuation—all emotion comes from it. Left on its own, it often leads us to act completely out of impulse. However, when you talk about what you're feeling, by necessity the feeling has to move from your amygdala to your prefrontal cortex, where your language and reasoning skills are born.

Go back to the film about the two boys shared in the Introduction (page 4). They had once been best friends but had not spoken in three months. These two boys, two of my favorites in the project, were able to gain power over something that was oppressing them by simply telling part of their story.

As an interviewer, providing a safe place to explore these feelings can be life-changing as individuals discover their own deep well of internal wisdom—and I would argue "eternal" wisdom. As I've said previously, just like we have a physiological immune system that automatically kicks into gear when we get a cut or a cold, I believe we also have a hidden emotional immune system that can cure 80% of our mental health challenges—but it is one that can only be unlocked by self-knowledge. This is why I say, *If knowledge is power, self-knowledge is superpower.* And that is how having the courage to tell our own story can guide us back to health.

NOT FEELING LIKE YOU ARE GOOD ENOUGH

This too is tied to the question of the source of self-worth. I am constantly mentoring bril-liant, high-achieving kids who never feel good enough—even though they are extraordinary. The problem is simple. They are worshiping at the altar of grades, or achievement, or popularity, or parental approval.

This does not stop with childhood. Adults, too, are seeking validation through climbing the ladder, pay grades, or approval from social groups and colleagues. The list goes on and on. Given that those are all sourced externally, they will be forever chasing a moving goal-line. Now ask yourself, who in their right mind would play a game with a moving goal-line? This is especially true of perfectionists who will never get to where they think they're going. This is a prescription for stress and frustration and burnout. The only way to combat it is to point out the folly of chasing a moving goal line and, in fact, the ultimate undesirability of perfection. After all, we connect more out of our weakness and

Dr. Rick Stevenson

"Achievement, like junk food, tastes great going down but is far from nourishing."

"A zero sum game where there are only winners and losers allows us to justify putting others down."

vulnerability than our strength. If they're going to worship at any altar, it should be at the altar of character. Character is internal, it's controlled by the individual, and it is ultimately more important than any achievement today, tomorrow, in five years, or fifty years from now.

The good thing is that when you get the individual to state their character strengths, they tend to realize that they've already made it. They are good enough as they are. This is not to diminish the importance of ambition, hard work, achievement, and competition. It's just realizing that worshiping those things will never result in filling the void within them.

KEEPING SCORE & FEAR OF FAILURE

If you think about it, we can only ever do the best that we can do. Hence, competition with others sets up yet another prescription for not feeling good enough—or the opposite. It sets up life as a zero-sum game where *winners* means there must be losers. This allows us to justify putting others down and keeping them there—or, on the contrary, being on the losing end of things. But if you think about it, the necessity of winning and losing is an artificial construct.

If you value winning, play against a bunch of first-graders. Now doesn't that feel good?

Life is more than keeping score

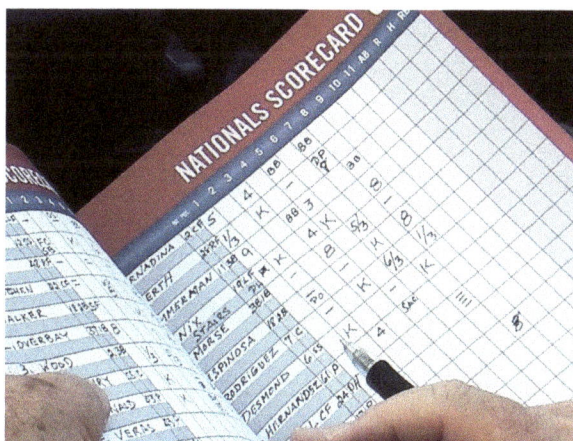

What if you play against your country's Olympics team? Should you feel worthless if you lose?

The fact of the matter is that sometimes you're going to win and sometimes you're going to lose. Quite frankly, *if you're not losing at least half the time, you're not challenging yourself enough.* You're chasing the first-graders. What's the answer? The answer is simple. Be competitive with yourself, not others. When you do the former, you always have a fair and accurate measuring stick and you don't set up all of life as a zero-sum game.

THE IMPACT OF SOCIAL MEDIA

We all know the problem. Social media can be a good connector, but over-consumption can also be a hugely destructive force. It leads to constant comparison, and huge swaths of teens admit to feeling worse about themselves and,

at times, even suicidal as a result. It does not help that what people are projecting is usually an embellishment if not an outright lie. Add the addictive factors and we have the perfect engine for self-destruction. I've had a few kids notice this and give up their Instagram accounts outright. And to a person, they end up empowered and much happier as a result. Others find it difficult to let go, however, and the best you can do for them is simply make them aware of the influences on them. They can then decide if they're going to keep taking the poison. Again, which wolf are they feeding?

RUMOR

Quite honestly, I don't have an answer for this one. Rumors are usually cruel and out of our control. When I was in high school I was student body president and I had a consistent rival who was quite brilliant, but also quite competitive with me for political office. There was a girl who just happened to be one of the only minority kids in our school—something that was no doubt difficult for her. She just happened to have a crush on this rival of mine who, as far as I know, did not return the interest.

About two years after I graduated, I was on a long car ride back from my college to Seattle with an acquaintance who had also been to my high school. As we bonded during the long drive, he said he wanted to ask me about something. Evidently when I was in my final year, a rumor went around that this minority girl had asked me to the Tolo (a formal dance where the girls ask the boys) and I had turned her down saying I would not be seen with her. The acquaintance said it didn't ring true to the person he was getting to know. Upon hearing this I practically crashed the car. Of course that never happened, but the thought of that rumor going around made me feel awful for months. When I got to the bottom of it, I discovered that the girl had wanted to ask my rival and had started the rumor so that my rival would say yes to going with her in response. I'm told it worked.

Today, given the existence of social media, I would have heard about the rumor right away and people would have come to their own conclusions in a nanosecond. It probably would have been worse. I empathize with those who suffer as a result of a malicious assault on their character. There is no justice in it.

The next year (1976), I got an internship working for my Senator in Washington DC. His name was Henry "Scoop" Jackson and he was a major contender running for president. An opposition book came out that was pure character-assassination and stooped so low as

— Henry "Scoop" Jackson

to attack his wife's hairdo among other personal things. In a quiet moment, I asked the senator how he put up with such things and if they hurt or not. I will always remember his answer. He replied, "Rick, it hurts deeply, especially when it involves my family. And I hope it never stops hurting. But that is the price we pay for a free press and a free press is what keeps us free."

Today, when rumors, falsehoods, conspiracy theories, and "alternative facts" are introduced as truth under the guise of news, it is even trickier. While a free press can be a watchdog for government and corporate abuse, alternately it can also allow people with ulterior motives a platform to lie and profit from it. The only thing we can do as a society is try to educate ourselves and our children in discerning fact from fiction and to take all rumors with a healthy grain of salt. As for us, the only thing we can do is to try to be the best versions of ourselves and live beyond reproach so as not to provide fuel to any accusation. But look at me… I'm still bothered by this high school rumor!

Is there any way to bring it back to helping the kid who has been the victim of a rumor? I would advise seeking out allies and trustworthy friends who have your back—friends and allies who can help counter the lies and set the record straight to whatever extent possible. At the end of the day, what is the personal impact? It can either cause grave injury and result in destructive things like suicide—or, alternatively, it can create a very resilient person who becomes stronger for it.

GRIEF, LOSS & DEATH

In my interviews, the topic of death does not come up more than any other—but the evidence of sorrow is almost always present.

Dr. Rick Stevenson

———————— *Fake news has been around a long time… since this 1894 political cartoon, if not before*

"We do not do a good job of teaching kids the role of sorrow in our lives."

This is true for adults who have lost a mate, a friend, or even a child. Or maybe it is something else hugely valuable to them. A business, a marriage, a childhood expectation.

For kids and teens, it normally arises around the death or sickness of a grandparent or a favorite pet. In fact, the latter often produces the most outpouring of sadness. This may be because the death of a pet represents a first-hand loss; but I also think the death of a pet—

or, to a similar extent, a grandparent—represents a safe, acceptable catch-all for all of the sorrow in a child's life.

I was recently interviewing a 16-year-old who was completely stoic when talking about his parents' recent divorce. The breakup had come somewhat out of the blue, and I knew that family had been the greatest priority in this young man's life—the thing for which he always felt most grateful. Yet he either could not or would not express his feelings about the divorce. I asked if he'd spoken to his brother and sister about it, and he had not. Even though they were all suffering a similar tragedy in the closest of proximity, they did not have the vocabulary to express their "sad," and comfort one another.

About the same time, however, his dog had been diagnosed with cancer and they had to put him down. He was very clear about his

The 5000 Days Project, Khun (Cambodia)

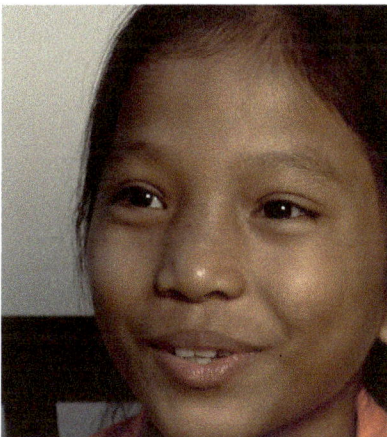

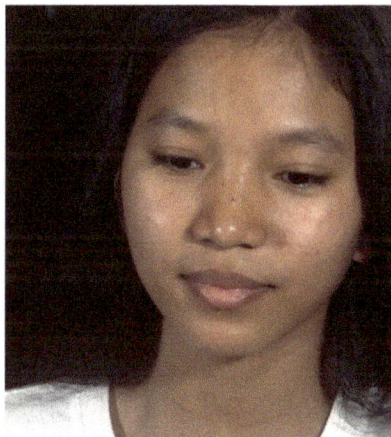

emotions surrounding this sad coincidence. I do believe that pets represent innocence, and hence the sadness surrounding losing them is uncomplicated. However, I also think that they become a conduit for everything sad and sorrowful in our lives.

Because sadness is perceived as a negative emotion—one that involves feelings we'd rather not feel, feelings that supposedly make us weak and vulnerable—my work with kids has made it clear that we do not do a good job of teaching kids the role of sorrow in our lives. Hence, they are either devastated by it or try to deny it. Either way, they are not processing it; and as long as they don't, it too will eat them like a cancer. Physically and emotionally.

To help kids process these feelings, I start by asking them something that seems obvious: Why are they sad? People and animals die every day. What is different here? Whether it is the death of a pet or a grandparent, the answer always gets down to "Because I loved them." While I'm not in the habit of quoting Winnie the Pooh, A. A. Milne's words always help introduce the beautiful side of sadness. To paraphrase, when Pooh loses someone he says, "Aren't I so lucky to have loved someone so much that it hurts so much when they're gone?"

Death or loss hurts because we're losing something special to us, something not everyone will have the privilege of experiencing. Feeling sadness is a way of honoring what we've lost.

Does that mean that pain is a by-product of loving something or someone? That there can be no joy without sorrow? What a powerful thing to watch children mature before my very eyes as they contemplate this. You can see the wheels turning, minds processing feelings they

— A. A. Milne

Dr. Rick Stevenson

> "Walking through this realization of fears with a perfectionist is one of the great pleasures of doing what I do."

have been trying to deny or ignore.

Whether the source of sorrow is a death or even a painful breakup, I ask them the ultimate question: "If you had a chance to never feel this pain again but also never feel the love that preceded it... or love again knowing that pain and sorrow is a part of it, what would you choose?" Nine out of ten kids choose the latter.

When I ask people about their greatest struggle, many say procrastination. Leaving things until the last moment makes their lives hell—and the same for their families. When asked if their lives would be better if they did not procrastinate, they universally say, "Yes."

However, when asked why they procrastinate, they often blame it on laziness. When asked to describe their schedules, a familiar answer is, "I wake up at 5:45 and go for a run. I'm out of the shower by 6:25, get dressed, eat breakfast, and get on the bus by 7:18. I go to my study group before classes or work begins and then..." After school or work the evening goes the same way. You get the picture. "You're just lazy" is a false narrative that they have bought into for lack of a better explanation. No wonder they cannot solve their procrastination problem when they are addressing it as an

Lesson Sixteen

> "People ultimately are what they do, not what they say."

issue of laziness. What's the answer? To make their life even busier. *No.*

The real answer? To get that, you need to identify the chief fear. Most procrastinators are perfectionists and, for a perfectionist, the chief fear is being imperfect. So, if a perfectionist leaves work until the last moment and does not earn a perfect score or result, the failure can be blamed on leaving the work until the last moment. By contrast, if a perfectionist completes work ahead of time and still fails to get a perfect score... well, that's imperfection, a real failure!

Walking through this realization of fears with a perfectionist is one of the great pleasures of doing what I do. In many cases perfectionists are brilliant, high-level achievers. Realizing that their less-than-perfect tendency to procrastinate is actually a product of their own fears and hence within their grasp to address is

a thrilling revelation for them.

LACK OF MOTIVATION & PRESSURES AT SCHOOL

Of course, not all procrastinators are perfectionists. Some are people who simply don't have the motivation to do what they're meant to do. This is a different problem.

There is a saying: "People vote with their feet." In other words, people ultimately are what they do, not what they say. If someone is not doing something they are meant to do, they simply don't want to do it badly enough to figure it out. This is again a result of "being out of tune with oneself"—a disconnect between who they are and what they truly want.

For kids, for instance, more often than not, it is difficult to get motivated when you don't see the connection between what you're taught in school and your future. "Why do I have to take

Einstein did not fail math, he learned to love it…

"Why learn military history if you are going to be a doctor? My answer: *Drop it.*"

trigonometry? I want to be a landscape designer. I can't get motivated. I hate math."

Of all of the things I hear in interviews, this is one of the most common. Math is usually the target—but English, social sciences, and languages take pretty good hits as well depending on the interests or strengths and weaknesses of the child.

And in many cases, this is a difficult question

to answer. Why take languages if you are committed to being a scientist? Why learn military history if you are going to be a doctor?

My answer? "Drop it." The student looks shocked. "What?" I enunciate for clarity, "Drop it. Drop math."

"Can I do that?" the student asks.

"Sure. I'm a big believer that you should never do what you don't want to do. Do you want to do math?" I probe.

"No," the student says. "But I need it for graduation. It's a requirement." "Oh, you want to graduate?" I ask. The student nods.

"Why? Lots of people don't graduate."

"Well, I want to get into a good university," the

———————— *Remember, we don't always make perfect choices (c.f. Bill Gates, below)*

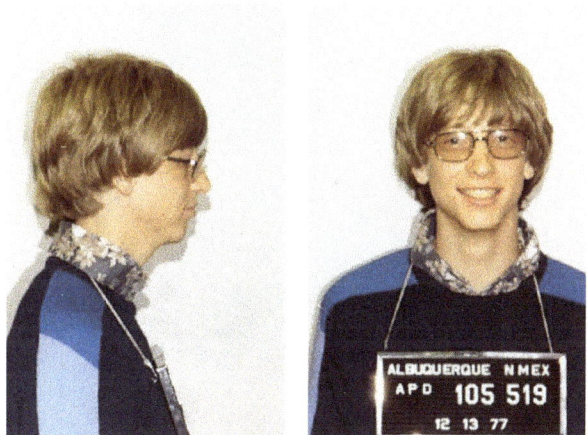

student says. "Why?" I ask. "Lot of people don't go to university."

"Well, I want to get into a good university so I can get a good job?" the student says, starting to question this line of inquiry.

"And what's your definition of a 'good' job? There are plenty of jobs."

The student asserts, "A 'good' job is one that I will enjoy going to every day. I don't want to have a job I hate."

"Why?" I ask again.

The student becomes a bit annoyed, "Because I want to have a happy life."

"Okay," I say. "Now let's reverse engineer that. You want to have a happy life... which requires you having a job you love, which means going to a good university, which means getting into a good university, which requires graduating from school—which involves taking math.

"So... You do want to do math, after all?"

The student looks at me confusedly, then slowly nods. This fact cannot be denied.

"And let me ask you another question. Currently, is your math homework ten times harder than your other homework because you hate it?" I ask.

"Yes. Absolutely."

"How would you like to make it ten times easier?" Another nod, suspiciously. "Your answer is simple. You may not think you like math but you have already decided you're going to do it because you want everything that comes from it. So you have two choices.

The dreaded math homework

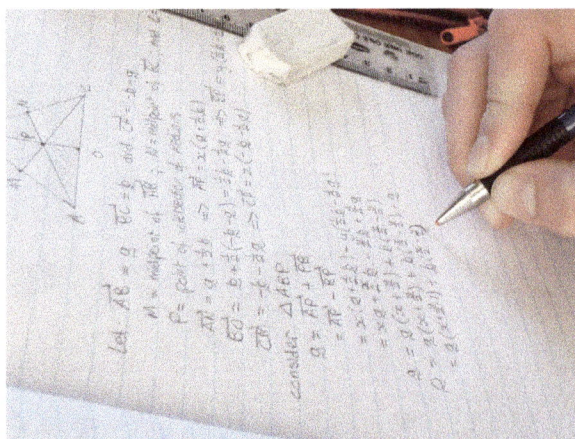

"When Oliver said he hated math, it was never about the math, really; he just hated feeling stupid."

You can hate it and continue feeling victimized; or you can try to find the love of it. As you know, there are at least two ways of looking at exactly the same thing. Because you are deciding not to make your peace with math, you make it ten times harder on yourself. Why would you possibly do that to yourself since you've already decided to take it? If you use your creativity to find the love of math, you not only make it ten times easier but you will learn how to turn things that victimize you into things you master."

Of course, it's never really that easy. This doesn't happen with a snap of the fingers. How do you "find the love" of something you don't inherently enjoy or find difficult?

A good and vital first step is finding the reasons behind the feeling. For instance, my son, Oliver, "hated math" and was always in "catch-up mode." Math and languages are particularly difficult because when you get even a tiny bit behind, you feel like you're a mile behind. Oliver is a smart kid and, like most of us, does not like the things that make him feel otherwise. We got him a tutor and now miraculously, he is enjoying it. When he said he "hated math," it was never about the math, really; he just hated feeling stupid.

We often say certain kids have a "head for math" or have a "head for social sciences."

The 5000 Days Project, Oliver (Canada)

Assuming some version of that is true, how do we find the love of something for which we don't "have a head"? The answer involves putting the question in a broader perspective. We need to look at the task as one of those "difficult things" that we will face in life; and if we can rewrite the challenge in our heads to rise above a particular difficult thing we will gain confidence in facing similar difficult things in the future. In other words... punt on math now, and you'll probably punt plenty of other things later. Learn to love math now... and that experience may later help you save your job, your marriage, or your relationships with your kids! That could really make me love math.

Another math story involves my daughter Leah who came home one day frustrated saying, "I have a math teacher who does not teach math." I said, "What?" She explained that he "just puts the book down in the middle of us all and says *figure it out.*" So during parent night I asked him about his method. He said, "Rick, it's simple. 90% of these kids will never use any of the math that I'm teaching them—it's at such a high level. However, I can teach them something they'll use every second of every day. Problem solving. If I can throw out something difficult and they bitch and moan and blame and accuse and then start to work together to find a solution, I have given them the ultimate life skill because, all of life is problem solving." Needless to say, I walked away in awe. That's teaching.

This is where our education system could learn from the way our brains actually work.

As this relates to adults, procrastination may involve perfectionism but it may also be a sign that they're simply having to do something that they hate doing. I always recommend that they listen to this sign and get rid of that

The 5000 Days Project, Leah (Canada)

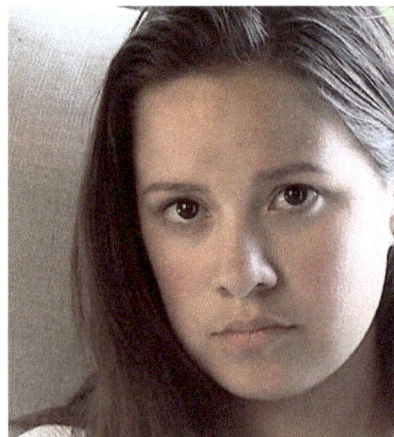

> # "In wealthier countries most kids look at school as a prison sentence, and the main reason they go is to see their fellow inmates."

requirement in their lives. In many cases they realize that that is not an option because it undermines a greater priority in their life. Being reminded of that connection often allows them to develop a new mindset around it.

SCHOOL & WORK: ATTITUDE VS. GRATITUDE

I have had the privilege of visiting hundreds of schools around the world. In the wealthier countries, most kids look at school as a prison

sentence, and the main reason they go is to see their fellow inmates. In poorer countries where the school systems have a fraction of the resources and advanced training, students are grateful for the chance to be educated. They see school as their passport to a brighter future. Despite the disparity, which environment do you think is more conducive to learning? If you guessed the latter, you are correct. Sadly, most of us grew up in the "have to go to school" versus the "get to go to school" environment. The effectiveness of our education system and general level of enthusiasm among youth would double in a day if we could rediscover the privilege of learning.

This attitude goes far beyond school. It applies to many of the jobs we end up landing as adults as well. All of advertising and social media in wealthier countries is constantly focusing on what we "lack" versus what we "have." Hence, it is no surprise that we kneel at

Gratitude = Better Learning

I want to be a nurse.

the altar of materialism worshiping false gods that will never satisfy our souls. I am always hearing the same take-away from American high school and college kids after they return home from doing a service trip abroad: "Those people have nothing but are so much happier than we are."

I find that most people, when reminded of their blessings versus their curses, are quickly capable of seeing their cups as half-full versus half-empty, no matter what their situation. I have gotten in the habit of wrapping up most interviews with questions such as "Finally, what are you most grateful for?" By sending them away with a focus on what they have versus what they don't (the simple key to happiness), you empower them with an outlook that will not only serve them well but will always be within their control.

Dr. Rick Stevenson

FEAR OF NOT BELONGING & LONELINESS

Most of us are fine with being alone but none of us want to feel alone. And we have all been there—whether it be feeling like the odd person out in our family, or being the new kid in school or on the job, scanning the lunch room for a place to sit. It's one of the worst feelings ever. Yet, we often bring it on ourselves. We accept it as being the lesser of two evils. We would rather feel alone than risk rejection, judgment, or vulnerability.

She sat in front of me, barely holding it together. At twelve years old, Ella was still the picture of innocence, but the secret she was about to share weighed heavily on her small, sloping shoulders. "I've been looking at porn," she whispered as the tears began to fall. "It just came up on my computer. I didn't look for it— but I looked at it. And I liked it." And then she broke into heavy sobs.

— The 5000 Days Project, Nikita (Russia)

"Drew, a straight-A student, football captain, wise beyond his years, still did not know how to process his friend's suicide."

After she was able to regain her composure, I asked her how liking porn made her feel. She said, "Kind of creepy, kind of good. Ashamed. Alone. Really alone.

"I'm close to my parents, but I could never tell them. I don't even know why I'm telling you."

"Maybe you're telling me because you don't want to feel alone," I suggested. "In fact, I think you want to tell your parents." She looked at me cautiously. "And, I think your parents would understand—because I can guarantee you that lots of kids, older and younger than you, have had this very experience."

She looked at me, shocked. "Really?" she said.

"Yes. What matters is what you decide to do from here."

Or take Drew, a gentle giant. Straight-A student, football captain, wise beyond his years, admired all around. When his good friend from childhood posted a suicide video and then killed himself with a shotgun as his parents entered the room, he was devastated. Despite the availability of grief counselors, Drew did not know how to process such a senseless act. Nor did his friends. He told me that, despite the availability of grief counselors,

The 5000 Days Project, Drew (USA)

after four months his close-knit group of friends were still not talking about it with each other. As a result, everyone felt even more alone.

And it's not just kids. Over half of our seniors report loneliness as one of their greatest struggles. In fact, the American Surgeon General found loneliness to have the negative health effects of smoking a pack of cigarettes a day—capable of taking as much as 15 years off of your life.

People tend to dwell in loneliness because despite being unhealthy, at least it seems to be a safe, familiar place. Safe from risk of rejection and judgment. We all know the stories of the people who have been physically abused that sometimes return to their abuser because at least it's familiar.

Every summer we run a storytelling program called the Prodigy Project (ProdigyCamp.org) which seeks to bring together 25 of the most talented teens in filmmaking and songwriting from around the world. The center of the camp is the campfire where kids come tasked with talking about the most difficult thing they've ever faced. The theory is that if they can tell the most difficult story they'll ever tell—their own—they will be able to tell any story. Everyone approaches the first campfire with dread. Being completely honest and vulnerable with a new group of people is the last thing they want to do. But the moment someone rises to the occasion, the flood gates open and within a few short hours, and over the course of the week, life-long relationships are established that sometimes surpass their best ones at home.

Adolescence creates the perfect storm of loneliness. Because of the changes happening within each teen, they suddenly feel too old to

Dr. Rick Stevenson

The 5000 Days Project, Jake (USA)

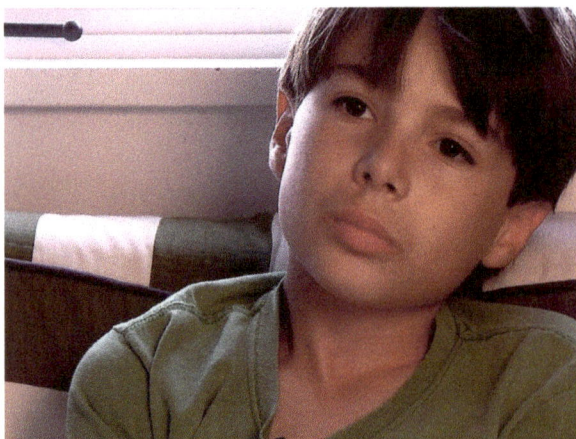

Watch our short film about Jake and his struggle with grief using this QR code.

tinyurl.com/storyq16

110

"Despite his many honors and achievements, in the end, my father only cared about one thing: relationships."

talk to their parents and too young to talk to each other. Hence, they feel like they are the only ones experiencing the doubts, fears, and insecurities they are feeling. Once they discover almost everyone else is feeling the same way, their world in one fell swoop suddenly feels a lot less lonely.

The good news is that most of us have a means to escape our loneliness if we're just willing to take a risk. Ninety-nine times out of a hundred, that risk pays off, rewarding us with the elixir of connection. Many of you will remember the Harvard happiness study where time and time again it affirmed that happiness comes not from wealth, position, or education but from connection.

Sure enough, in the final months of his life, as my dad was dying from cancer, he gave me the greatest gift a father could give a son. He gave me the gift of knowing ultimately what counts. Despite his many honors and achievements, in the end, my father only cared about one thing —his relationships.

So, this is what I recommend for those who are struggling with loneliness. Discover the fear; call it out and see if it's really that serious. Fear of rejection is normally a projection. We project our own insecurities on others and anticipate their disapproval. In fact, we may find ourselves pushing off intimacy and

— Dr. William G. Stevenson

rejecting others first just to avoid the anticipated result. This mindset is the breeding ground for loneliness.

However, if we're willing to risk rejection, we seldom have to suffer it. If we do get rejected, at least we've been empowered by the effort because we've dared to be courageous. I find that with most people, loneliness is a self-fulfilling prophecy. To paraphrase Henry Ford, if someone says they can't do something, they're normally right.

Most of it is internal. The person who is out of tune with themselves will likely feel alone even in a crowd. A person who is in tune with themselves will likely be in tune with their surroundings and will not feel alone even if they're entirely on their own.

To me, this gets to the heart of the interview. The truth of the matter is that most people are reluctant to tell their story. It makes them feel too vulnerable. However, when they take the risk, they are almost always, without exception, grateful you took them there.

FAMILY ISSUES

Time and time again, when kids are asked what they are most grateful for, *Family* is the answer. This is true even if the family is dysfunctional. We don't get to choose our families but we don't give up on them easily either. They can be the source of great joy or tremendous misery.

Again, one of my first sets of questions has to do with family. "Describe each member using just one word." This is a great way to see what dynamics might be at work. Going through the one-word descriptions helps the individual gain perspective on the relationships they have with each one of them. Subjects range from

The 5000 Days Project, siblings Baer & Charley / Tristan & Camryn

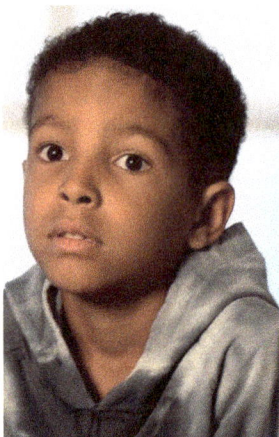

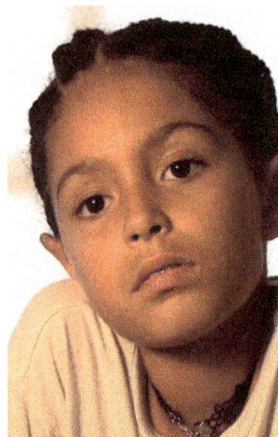

> ## "Siblings are often the prime instigator of an individual's anger, but when I ask if they'd like a better relationship they usually answer *yes.*"

The most common description of a troublesome sibling is "annoying." Those siblings are also often the prime instigator of the individual's anger. I ask if they'd like a better relationship. They usually answer yes. I then ask what they think it would take—or what that would look like. It often involves them demanding that the offending sibling simply be less annoying. I then ask for specifics—how they are annoying, and what they think that sibling wants. They normally get to the conclusion that they want attention.

Remember the story I told about our adopted daughter, Leah, at three years old? Despite not wanting to encourage her annoying behavior, we faced it head on, gave her what she really needed, and it solved the problem.

The interviews I do often involve kids whose greatest fear is disappointing their parents. These kids often are high achievers. If the fear

how well they get along with siblings to dealing with the expectations of parents.

Believe it or not, family is so important that most kids truly want a better relationship. It's often a matter of acknowledging patterns and giving them perspective on the inexplicable forces that often victimize us.

The 5000 Days Project, siblings Edison & Princeton

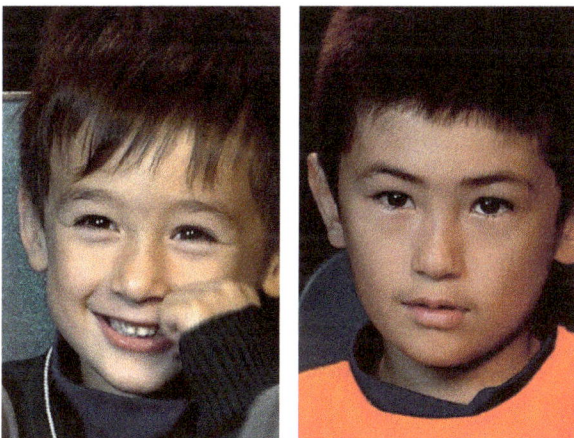

For a look at family dynamics, watch our short film about Sam and Luke.

tinyurl.com/storyq17

of disappointing parents is the primary motivator, it all eventually goes south at some point as the child starts to separate. The goal here is to wean the child off whatever need they have to impress their parents and get them to own their own motivations. While there is the occasional so-called "Tiger" or "Helicopter" parent, much of the fear the child has is really of disappointing themselves. They just blame it on their parents. Most parents these days are pretty tuned into the negative effects of stress on their kids. If the child is blaming their parents, I ask if they fail at something, would the parent stop loving them? The answer is almost always "no." Then I ask if they would stop loving themselves—and the answer is revealing.

Sometimes, I deal with a child's predicament where a parent is failing them. This may involve narcissism or absenteeism. In those cases, it's helpful to acknowledge that we are not all dealt a fair hand in the family we inherit.

I know of one case where the father had a substance abuse problem and was stealing from his son. While the son could not control the type of father his father was, he could control the type of son he wanted to be. His choice was to have a relationship but with very strong boundaries especially surrounding money. He could have just walked away, but this boy wisely knew that if he did that, he would be the one left with a hole in his life. He managed to take a victimizing situation and learn how to be the master of it.

GLOBAL WARMING, RACISM, HUNGER, POVERTY, INJUSTICE

As previously stated, near the end of each interview I ask for the individual's three wishes. This goes for all ages.

Wikipedia explains helicopter parents

Dr. Rick Stevenson

"World peace begins at the cellular level—it begins with each one of us."

Again, up until age 12, the most common answer is "World Peace." The second concern of most young people is global warming followed by racism, hunger, poverty, injustice, and so on. Despite their young ages, these kids have minds weighed heavily by these issues. As they grow older, the wish for world peace starts to dwindle, however, as individuals feel like it sounds naive. My doctoral thesis focused on world peace.

I concluded there was not a systematic political, economic, religious, or social solution—and I'm an optimist. But I had a *big* realization when a friend shared this familiar thought attributed to the ancient Chinese philosopher, Lao Tzu. To paraphrase, he said: if there is going to be peace between nations, there first needs to be peace within nations; but before there is peace within nations, there first needs to be peace within communities; but before there is peace between communities, there first has to be peace within families; but before there is peace within families, there first must be peace within our own hearts. In other words, world peace begins at the cellular level—it begins with each one of us.

These concerns are huge and could easily be disempowering. I have found, however, something encouraging. When you get individuals to start at home with themselves,

The 5000 Days Project, Boston (USA)

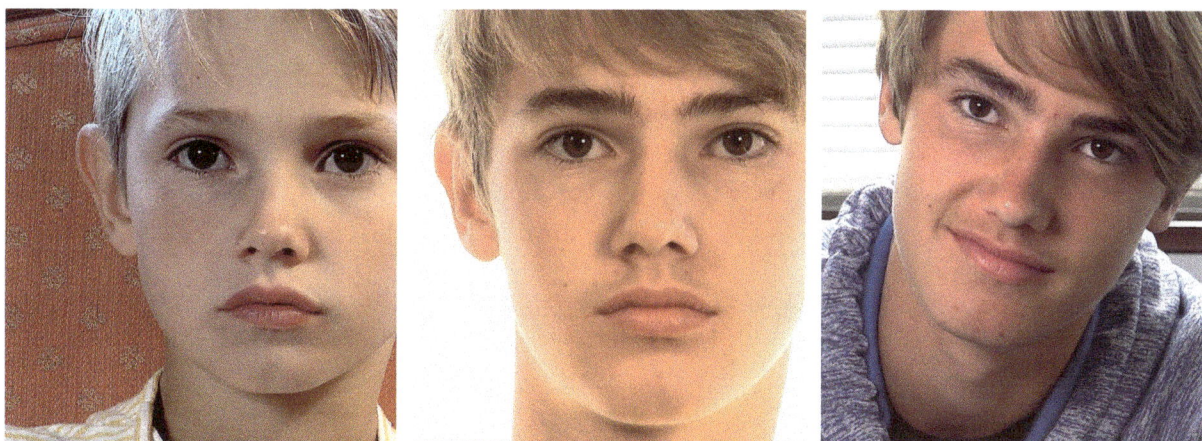

and you encourage them to be the best version of themselves, they not only walk away empowered, but can set a course of activism where they can make a difference. One of the most promising things about the way we are raising our kids these days is that many of them have a cause and ambition to create a better world. We have taught them to care.

FOMO—FEAR OF MISSING OUT

FOMO is the ultimate teen disease. One of the blessings of the pandemic is that FOMO temporarily went away—because no one was doing anything in groups that led others to fear they were missing out.

I interviewed one girl who—despite being brilliant, athletic, popular, and multi-talented—was constantly concerned that she was being excluded, or that she was missing out. During the pandemic, she had to confront her ultimate fear, which she discovered was being alone with herself. The pandemic gave her time to actually learn to love herself and as we came back to some degree of "normal," she matured past the problem.

But it still will arise, and you as an interviewer are there to help the individual discover why they're so "thirsty." That discussion is really revealing—why they need to be in the center of action in order to feel validated or valued.

In the adult world, FOMO is much less present. That said, it does tend to drive middle-age crises and often gets people in trouble. Restlessness is the most common indicator. The best way to deal with it is to talk through priorities and reexamine values.

Dr. Rick Stevenson

The 5000 Days Project, Poppy (Australia)

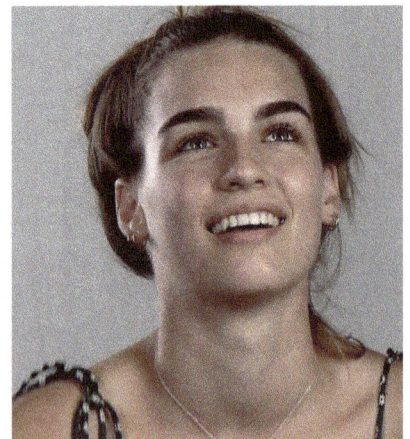

116

"Holding on to hatred is like taking poison and expecting the other person to die."

BULLYING

Bullying, like rumors, is an injustice often beyond the individual's control. Sometimes the individual can deal with it by just walking away.

Another option involves robbing the bully of the reaction they might be seeking. However, sometimes, it simply has to be reported. No kid wants to be a snitch—a sad tradition that keeps bullies in power. However, you can be the ear they need in order to develop a strategy.

You can also help them get free of the emotional torment that often follows victims of bullying for years. This can be achieved, strangely, by building empathy for the bully—asking them what influences they think the bully has suffered that makes them the way they are. This is relevant to adults as well because people are bullied at all ages. Eventually, you will want to help the individual adopt a "forgive if not necessarily forget" mindset. After all, forgiveness is primarily for the forgiver. Anything else is counter-productive and just prolongs the control the bully has over the traumatized individual. As the Buddhist proverb goes, "Holding on to hatred is like taking poison and expecting the other person to die."

The 5000 Days Project, Arvind (USA)

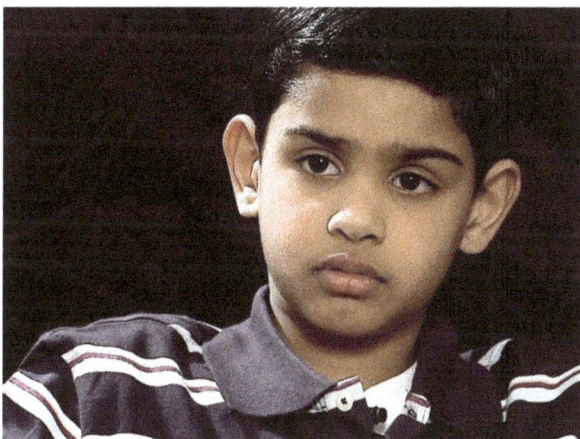

Watch one of our short films which addresses bullying using this QR code.

tinyurl.com/storyq18

SUICIDAL THOUGHTS

Suicidal thoughts seem to rise when the perceived pain of living is greater than the perceived pain of dying. I think almost everyone has thought about it at one time or another. The problem is when these thoughts become normalized and plans are being made. This an area where you are likely to want to be helpful and bring in help as well—such as parents, or the suicide help line 988.

Being helpful means helping the individual get to the source of this pain, and getting help means making sure the right people are informed if the situation merits it.

I had a situation where one of the boys from the Prodigy Camp called me one January. He said he needed to share something with me but would do so only if I was sworn to secrecy. I had little choice but to agree. He admitted he had made an attempt on his own life with pills. I knew he did not talk to his parents and that it was a difficult relationship at best. I was also leaving to film in Australia later that week. I was not sure what to do. If it meant saving his life, I was not beyond breaking my word.

However, a better idea emerged. I sent out a note to the local Prodigy Campers and, on short notice, we pulled together a campfire for those who could make it. Despite a snowfall, every local kid made it and the boy was able to share his situation with the group. Coincidentally, another boy in the group had been having similar thoughts and both were able to share. The group then became the support for these two boys and the crisis soon passed as kids vowed to reach out and check in.

Another effective thing I have seen work is the acknowledgement that suicide is just passing

SAVE THE NUMBER
SAVE A LIFE
CALL OR TEXT 988

988
SUICIDE & CRISIS LIFELINE

Add this number to your phone now.
It could save a life later.

National Institute of Mental Health

nimh.nih.gov/suicideprevention

Dr. Rick Stevenson

> # "Even the toughest of heroes—and us— are reduced to frightened children when it comes to truly confronting our feelings."

on the pain. Often, an effective deterrent—beyond getting to the heart of the problem—is the person's reluctance to do that to their family and friends. Obviously, passing on hurt can also be the *objective* for some deeply damaged kids, so use this with discretion. It may also help to remind them that all of us have had the feeling, and all of us are grateful we did not act on it when the feeling passed.

VULNERABILITY, INSECURITY & WEAKNESS

I have a young girl in the project who is a sponsored athlete. She's quite incredible in almost every way and is not afraid to attempt death-defying stunts. However, when cracks in her once-stable family emerged, nothing was more frightening to her than the thought of actually talking about her feelings.

Indeed, as previously discussed, both Western and Eastern literature is full of the rough, tough, rugged individualist who silently suffers resiliently through disappointment, hurt, and tragedy. Certainly, there are times when just pushing through our difficulties is the only rational alternative. That said, even the toughest and more courageous of these characters—and us—are reduced to frightened children when it comes to truly confronting our feelings. In fact, as previously mentioned, we all "take bullets" every day and, if at some

— Rick mentoring Will (Australia)

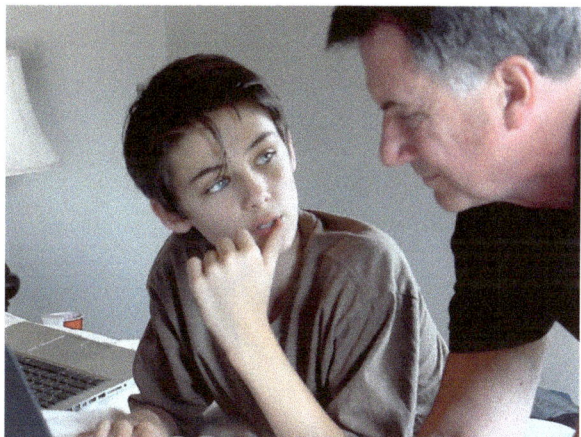

point, we don't stop to operate—by processing those feelings—we just end up bullet-ridden. No wonder our society is sick.

We are frightened of our feelings because they present an unpredictable landscape, one that makes us feel vulnerable. Yet once we dare to confront and process those feelings, we are relieved of the fear that paralyzes us, that keeps us quivering in the darkness. When we dare to acknowledge and name our feelings, we gain control over them. In fact, we learn that despite their unpredictable nature, those feelings are the one thing that let us know what's going on inside. They're a divining rod to the truth. They're an early warning system that, if heeded, can save us from greater hurt and harm down the road.

Our son Oliver is a proud introvert. Despite playing flashy misunderstood characters on his school's stage like Lord Farquaad in *Shrek* or Chip Tolentino in *The 25th Annual Putnam County Spelling Bee*, he is happiest at home as a house cat. Hence, when the call went out at his school for anyone interested in running for Prefect (student leadership), he had zero interest. Unlike his dad in school, he didn't need it, nor did he want it. However, he is passionate about questions of tolerance and kindness so when I asked him what he'd do if he was elected, he was quite outspoken. When I encouraged him to think about doing something about it, I could see the wheels reluctantly turning. And, as his father, I was so convinced that it would be perfect for him, I was not above offering an incentive. The only problem was that at his excellent, yet highly competitive school, almost half the class had signed up to run. With thirty kids running, they were each given only sixty seconds to state their platform. Oliver emerged with the following speech.

The 5000 Days Project, Cambodia

Dr. Rick Stevenson

"I am going to be brutally honest. I am often insecure. There are times where I feel as if I don't measure up to others. I'm not a vibrant social butterfly, I'm not top of the class, and oftentimes I lack confidence and care way too much about what others think. I'm scared of truly being myself, in fear that people won't like what they see.

"I'm saying all of this because I believe that some of you may feel the same way and that maybe, if we dare to be a little more honest and vulnerable with one another, we could create an even kinder place."

He won a Prefect spot and he did so on his own terms. He said, "Dad, it's so simple. We connect much more out of our vulnerabilities than our strengths." Indeed. My experience is that when as an interviewer you give your interviewee a safe place to talk about their strengths and weaknesses, their insecurities and their vulnerabilities—and you're willing to do the same—you free them from a lifetime of fear while building a deep connection.

AN UNCERTAIN FUTURE

In the wake of a worldwide pandemic, I think we, as a species, are struggling with the increasingly unstable, unpredictable nature of life. As human beings, we hate uncertainty. We hate lack of predictability. We hate change. We want to know that we'll be safe, and know exactly where our next meal is coming from. We want to know that if we work hard and get a good education, we can make enough money to build a house with doors, windows, and walls that will help keep out unpredictable things. Walls that more often than not make us feel even more isolated and alone.

If you go out in the country far enough to escape city light pollution and look up at the

The 5000 Days Project, Cambodia

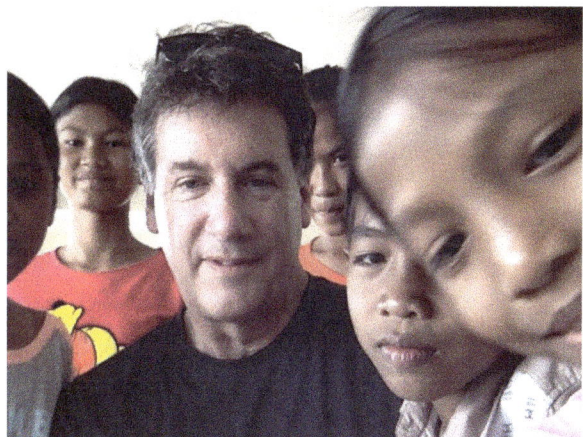

"Change is happening all around us, all the time. Change is actually the nature of things."

Dr. Rick Stevenson

moon and the stars, you see a universe that is vast, cold, and seemingly static. But your eyes are deceiving you because our human eyes have difficulty capturing transformation. We see things in snapshots. When you bring in a time-lapse camera, you realize that actually something incredible is happening before your very eyes—you see that the world is spinning at 1000 miles an hour, that stars are dying and being reborn. The Universe is expanding and constantly in the act of creation. That's when you realize that *change is happening all around us… that change is actually the nature of things*—NOT predictability. And that you are part of that everlasting, ever-changing NOW.

So how do we help others deal with the future as a major source of stress? The key is to help them develop an entirely new relationship with change—changing their mindset to view it not as a threat but as an opportunity—one that they know we can handle. To paraphrase Charlie Wardle, "The confidence a bird has lies not in the strength of the branch on which it sits, but in its ability to fly." I believe we can fly…

And taking a further cue from our ever-evolving universe, if we're writing our own story, we too have an opportunity to evolve day by day, on the road to becoming the best version of ourselves. After all, through every action, every thought, every moment of every

Our expanding universe

day we are writing our autobiography in real time. Knowing that, the best way to deal with an uncertain future is to create it.

None of us own anything more valuable than our own story. We may currently be the product of our past but we have the opportunity to be the Authors of our Future.

The following is a Quick Start guide for both virtual and in-person interviews—covering everything from the pre-interview process, equipment checks, and the interview script through post-interview process and backing-up files, with step-by-step suggestions. From these we recommend creating a checklist template you can tailor for use in each interview you conduct.

Customer Outreach. StoryQ has spent more than a decade establishing a network of parents and families incentivized to expand their Emotional Intelligence via Personal Story Mentoring. Our technology has allowed school children a taste of the approach through our automated StoryQ "StoryCatcher" (and related web apps), so parents and graduating children alike are already aware of the power of the StoryQ Method. This has been an effective method of outreach as access to children and their families normally takes a school or organization to back the Method and bring it to the attention of busy families. So many express regret that they did not sign up and start their child earlier. Getting the school's formal nod of approval through offering up the program is constantly named as the other reason parents feel secure signing their kids up.

If you work through StoryQ as a Personal Story Mentor, you may never need to worry about outreach as StoryQ will likely bring subjects to you. Word of mouth is likely your most effective tool of engagement—which is encouraging, because it's the best and cheapest form of promotion: parents talking to other parents or kids talking to other kids. The cost of advertising is, by comparison, cost-prohibitive and is unlikely to get you past the primary barrier to entry: the inherent reluctance people have to sitting down in front of a camera. People are more likely to drop their guard when the offer comes from an individual or organization they already trust.

The same is true of outreach for adult interviews. CEOs talking to other CEOs, for instance, sell the corporate experience. Individuals interested in self-help do the same. And again, StoryQ's established network of corporate services can bring business directly to you. Independent Mentors would be wise to cultivate their own networks of business and self-help leaders to generate leads.

Customer Contact. Typically, customers contact us through the StoryQ website (StoryQ.com), school websites, or the 5000 Days Project website. It is essential that the contact and registration process be automated. For StoryQ, our Project Administrators simply monitor emails for registration and audition notifications, and then forwards details to the appropriate StoryQ department.

From there, the assigned Mentor assumes responsibility for direct contact with the registrant or family head—up until the point of billing, at which point Bookkeeping takes over. Post-billing, Project Administrators again handle occasional customer queries.

Prep for Child Interviews. Armed with registration details, StoryQ Mentors have access to a central database where they can attach their own notes. They then email the parents/guardians for two reasons.

First, for scheduling. We agree on a mutual time. If it's in the context of a school, we tell the parent it will happen automatically when the school assigns a time. Otherwise, we generally use an online scheduling system such as Calendly to book open PSM slots.

Second, we typically include the following paragraph in an email to the parents: "I always find that I conduct the most successful interviews when I have the insights only a parent can give as to their child's dreams, ambitions, struggles, and fears. If you have time could you email me a short paragraph passing on your insights?" The notes which the family provides are then also added to the central database. (StoryQ uses AirTable, which provides online team access and customizable views and forms for data entry.)

Prep for Adult Interviews. The StoryQ process for our adult interviews is similar to that for children—just tailored to adult input regarding dreams, ambitions, struggles, and fears. For Taking Stock or similar check-ins, the subjects themselves can often provide a preliminary self-assessment. For "Legacy" and family interviews, other family members can provide valuable insight.

The Audition/Interview. As mentioned in the training materials, a first interview for longitudinal Mentoring is considered a mutual audition for fit. Otherwise it works just the same as a regular PSM interview. Whether on Zoom or in person, you greet each individual and help them feel not only comfortable but also feel your excitement in catching up with them. Ideally, you are technically prepared by the time they arrive, but an audio and focus test is always in order. Personally, I have them test by saying, "Say, *Hey Rick how are you?*" After the sound checks I say, "I'm fine. Thanks for asking." That cheap trick normally makes them smile. I then say, "So, Michael, what's your name?" This relaxes them further and provides an audio ID on each film—in addition to the media labeling. You want to make sure the editor is looking at the right footage, "operating on the right patient." Then proceed with the questions you have selected as described in the training materials (Appendix B, below).

The Script. Be sure that your script for the interview includes more than just the interview questions themselves. Introduce yourself and your background, briefly, and let the interviewee know this is an audition, if that is the case, and what that means. Remind your interviewees that your goal is learning from them what it's like for them to experience their own life—to learn their story, the most important thing they own. Provide an estimate of how long the session might last. Set expectations in a fashion such that expectations can be satisfactorily met. You want this to be a good and rewarding experience.

The Privacy Guarantee. The single most important part of the interview is essentially the PSM version of Miranda Rights, tailored as appropriate for your interviewee: "Everything you say to me is private. Your parents have signed off on that guarantee. The only reason

that might change is if I think your or someone else's safety might be threatened. Then I will let you know and we'll make a plan together." When any interviewee is guaranteed privacy, they feel much freer to speak their truth, and it dramatically increases the chance the interview will help them.

Confirm that the subject looks and sounds great. Make final adjustments to lighting your subject, as needed, and check the position of the camera and subject one last time.

Then, confirm you are RECORDING. (Yes, this deserves its own line in the checklist!)

Have fun and ask away. Be sure you have reviewed your question list just prior to the session so that your focus can be on your subject rather than the list itself. Leave plenty of space for thoughtful responses, making an effort to not "lead the witness" by finishing sentences for them or putting words in their mouth.

I typically conclude on the most positive of notes—asking them what they're grateful for, or a favorite memory. I then ask whether we have covered everything they'd like to cover. I will often ask them how the interview was for them. Leaving things positive is essential as your subjects will remember their final feelings —the so-called "peak-end" bias, a clinically proven effect in which a person's perspective on an experience is heavily influenced by the best-or-worst and final moments, the "peak" and "end." You are in control of the end moment; take advantage of that.

Interview Conclusion. After concluding the question set, set expectations for follow-up steps as applicable. For example, for auditions, when will they find out if they are accepted into the longitudinal PSM program? What will the frequency be of interviews, and what is the final product? Provide scheduling details.

Post Interview Process. Update the central database with whatever notes you have recorded, other important reminders for yourself, and date of the next interview (if scheduled). File your recorded footage according to established protocols—which you must have nailed down in advance. The footage is the family jewels, and you cannot take chances with informal systems for handling. For StoryQ, we back up the footage in triplicate—local storage, cloud backup, and central archives. To prevent losing vital footage, we have found WeTransfer to be most effective in moving large files.

Finally, be sure the details of the session—date and completion—are recorded in the central database.

Post-Interview Follow-Up. Reply to the appropriate parties with status of the interview—and acceptance into the Program for auditions. (As mentioned in Lesson Seven, page 34, you may occasionally find that trying again in another year or two may be the recommendation.) Confirm the scheduling for next interview, as appropriate. Include a few impressions from the initial interview along with a few screen grab images for their enjoyment.

Whiz through the footage and pull out screen shots and color-correct them. Given that you'll have tens of thousands of frames to choose from, it only takes 5 minutes to find 3-4 thoughtful shots. Those shots often become the screen saver on their parent's computer. It becomes the perfect gift to parents and takes very little time.

Wording for Audition Follow-Up
It was a pleasure auditioning Robert for the 5000 Days Project today. I am happy to welcome him to the project and look forward to being his Personal Story Mentor as he grows. I'm copying my colleague Monique who will take care of your final paperwork and billing.

Wording for an Annual Interview
It was a pleasure seeing Robert for his annual 5000 Days Project today. I love his energy…

(and so on). Here are some screen grabs from the interviews. I'm copying my colleague Monique who will take care of your final paperwork and billing. Until next time…

B-Roll. For PSM contracts that include filming of personal background footage, I will also sometimes arrange a time with the family to film this "B-roll" at their house. I have the child give me a room tour introducing their stuff, sharing their arts and crafts. I also like to grab a little footage with parents or siblings interacting as it's almost always revealing.

Additional Post-Process for Corporate Clients. Unlike 5000 Days projects, here you're likely turning around the footage within the same month you've shot the interview. The goal is to trim the overall interview down to its basics and then do a shorter, public cut. Both go to the client for their approval before anyone else sees it. It may take going back and forth a time or two but should not take much more. After all, this is not a "documentary film." It's a condensed version of their own words. Once you've got an approved cut you can ask for any photos they'd like to add within limits you set. The goal is to send them away with something that makes them happy, something they can give as a gift to their family.

APPENDIX B: MASTER LISTS OF QUESTIONS FOR KIDS

AGES 4-6, CORE QUESTIONS

- ☐ What is your name and how old are you?
- ☐ What do you want to be when you grow up?
- ☐ Good job! Now tell me: Do you have a nickname? If so, how did you get it?
- ☐ Do you have any pets? Describe them. What are their names and what do you like about them?
- ☐ What do you get in trouble for the most?
- ☐ Who loves you?
- ☐ Describe each member of your family using just one word.
- ☐ What do you like most about yourself?
- ☐ What makes you happy?
- ☐ What makes you sad?
- ☐ What makes you angry?
- ☐ Now remember, this is private. Tell me when somebody has said something that hurts your feelings. What did they say?
- ☐ When was the last time you cried over something emotional and why?
- ☐ If you had three wishes, what would you ask for?
- ☐ Do you think it's easier to be a boy or girl? Why?
- ☐ Do you have an imaginary friend? If so, tell us about that friend?
- ☐ Who is your best friend and why?
- ☐ Do you ever have any scary dreams, or nightmares? If so, which one was the worst? What happened in it?
- ☐ If you had three wishes, what would you wish for? And no, you cannot wish for more wishes.
- ☐ If you could have one superpower, what would it be and why?
- ☐ Is there anything else you'd like to talk about today? Now is your chance.

EXTRA QUESTIONS

- ☐ Do you believe in God? If so, what do you think God looks like?
- ☐ What is the best present you've ever received?
- ☐ If you could know one thing about your future what would it be?

AGES 7-9, CORE QUESTIONS

☐ What is your full name and how old are you?

☐ Now think for a moment. On a scale of 1 -10, how are you feeling today? With one meaning miserable and 10 being super happy. Tell me why you are feeling this way.

☐ Do you have a nickname? If so, tell me the story behind how you got it.

☐ Describe each member of your family using one world (ie. Mom "Loving").

☐ Tell me a story about one or both of your parents.

☐ What do you want to do when you grow up?

☐ What do you like most about yourself?

☐ What do you need to work on?

☐ What makes you happy? For instance, if you could spend the perfect day, what would you be doing?

☐ What makes you angry? Give me an example.

☐ Have you ever been bullied or did someone call you a name you didn't like? Did you tell someone?

☐ What's one of your most embarrassing moments?

☐ When is the last time you cried from being sad and why?

☐ What is the hardest or most difficult thing that you've ever had to deal with?

☐ If you had three wishes (and no, you can't wish for more wishes), what would you ask for?

☐ What do you like most and least about the way you look?

☐ On a scale of 1-10, how happy are you overall?

☐ If you could change one thing about your life, what would that be?

☐ What's something that nobody else knows about you?

☐ If you could have one superpower, what would it be and why?

☐ Do you worry about anything when you lie awake at night? What is it?

☐ Are you in love? Do you have a crush on someone? If so, who? And do they know?

☐ Who loves you?

☐ If you had three wishes, what would you wish for? And no, you cannot wish for more wishes.

☐ Is there anything else you'd like to share about yourself or your life right now? Now's your chance.

Dr. Rick Stevenson

EXTRA QUESTIONS

- [ ] How do you think other people see you? If they were to describe you, what would they say?
- [ ] Tell me about a time when someone said something to hurt your feelings.
- [ ] Do you believe in God? If you pray, what do you pray for?
- [ ] Do you think is it easier to be a boy or a girl? Why?
- [ ] Who is your best friend and why?
- [ ] What would you most like to know most about your future?
- [ ] On a scale of 1-10, how happy have you been this year, with 10 being the happiest?
- [ ] Do you ever have any scary dreams, or nightmares? If so, which one was the worst? What happened in it?
- [ ] When have you lost someone or something meaningful to you that caused deep sorrow?
- [ ] If you had a chance to never feel this pain again but also never feel the love that preceded it... or love again knowing that pain and sorrow is a part of it, what would you choose?
- [ ] What are you most grateful for?

The 5000 Days Project, siblings Edward & Gaga

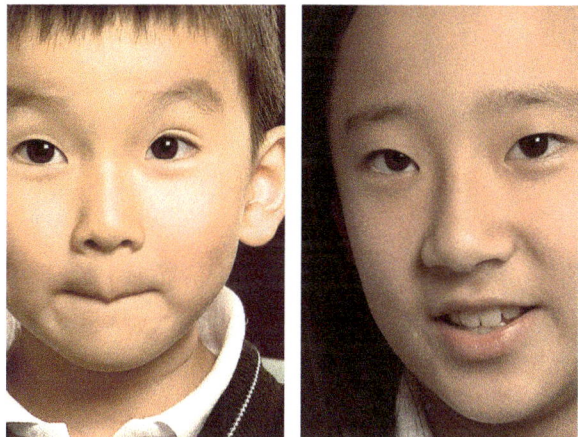

AGES 10-12, CORE QUESTIONS

- What is your full name and how old are you?
- Now think for a moment. On a scale of 1-10, how are you feeling today? With 1 meaning miserable and 10 being super happy. Tell me why you are feeling this way.
- What do you want to do when you grow up?
- Describe each member of your family using one word.
- Describe yourself in one word and tell me why you choose that word.
- What do you like most about yourself?
- What do you need to work on?
- What makes you really happy? For instance, if you could spend the perfect day, what would you be doing?
- What makes you angry? Give me an example.
- When was the last time you cried because you were sad and why?
- What's the most emotionally painful thing that has happened to you in your life?
- What's your happiest childhood memory? Where were you, who were you with, and what were you doing?
- If you had three wishes (and no, you can't have more wishes), what would you ask for?

- On a scale of 1-10, how happy are you overall?
- What do you like most and least about the way you look?
- Do you have a crush? If so, who are they, and do they know you feel that way about them?
- What is something most people don't know about you?
- If you could change one thing about the way kids treat each other, what would it be?
- If you could be invisible for a day at school, what would you do?
- What are you most grateful for?
- If you could have one superpower what would it be and why?
- When was the last time you lied and why?
- Do you worry about anything when you lie awake at night? What is it?
- Now try to go deeper... What do you think your greatest fear is in life?
- If you had three wishes, what would you wish for? And no, you cannot wish for more wishes.
- If you could change one thing about your life, what would it be and why?
- If for some reason, you could not see your family again, what would you want to say to them?

- ☐ If you could give yourself some advice ten years from now, what would it be? Go ahead and say it, directly into the camera to your future self.
- ☐ Is there anything else you'd like to share about you or your life right now? Now's your chance.

EXTRA QUESTIONS

- ☐ On a scale of 1-10, rate yourself in terms of looks.
- ☐ How are you with peer pressure?
- ☐ Do you believe in God? If so, how do your beliefs impact your daily life?
- ☐ Tell me about an embarrassing moment.
- ☐ What would you most like to know most about your future?
- ☐ What's your worst habit?
- ☐ What's your nerdiest characteristic?
- ☐ What is something you feel guilty about? Tell the story and remember this is completely private.
- ☐ Describe your perfect future 20 years from now. Where do you live? What are you doing? Are you married? Do you have kids?
- ☐ Most people have an embarrassing story about when they first found out how babies were made. Where were you, who told you, and what was your reaction?

The 5000 Days Project, siblings Paris & Weston

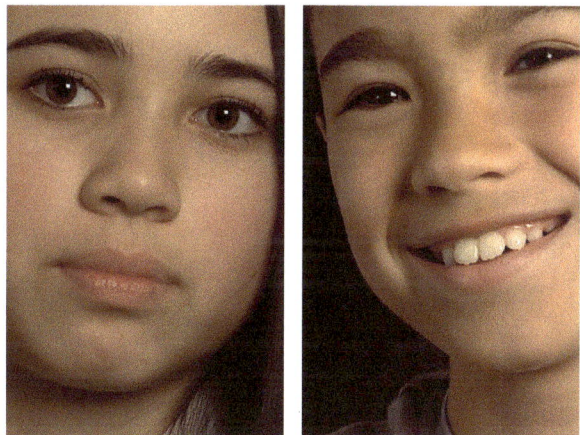

AGE 13, CORE QUESTIONS

- ☐ What is your full name and how old are you?
- ☐ Now think for a moment. On a scale of 1-10, how are you feeling today? With one meaning miserable and 10 being super happy. Tell me why you are feeling this way.
- ☐ What do you want to do when you grow up? And if you don't know specifically, try to remove all practical considerations. Your ultimate dream.
- ☐ What have you learned about yourself or about life this year?
- ☐ What do you think your best qualities are? I'm not talking about what you do. I'm talking about who you are.
- ☐ What do you need to work on?
- ☐ What makes you really happy? For instance, if you could spend the perfect day, what would you be doing?
- ☐ What makes you angry and why? Give an example.
- ☐ Who's your closest friend and why are they your closest friend?
- ☐ Have any of your friends or schoolmates ever said or done anything that hurt you or made you feel bad? What happened and what did you do?
- ☐ When was the last time you cried due to sadness and why?

- ☐ What's the most emotionally difficult thing you've ever had to face?
- ☐ Describe each member of your family using only one word for each... including yourself.
- ☐ What is the most frustrating thing about your parents/guardians? Is there something you want to do differently when you're a parent/guardian?
- ☐ What is one of your happiest childhood memories? Where were you, what were you doing and with whom?
- ☐ If you had three wishes (and no, you can't wish for more wishes), what would you ask for?
- ☐ On a scale of 1-10, how happy are you overall?
- ☐ If you could snap your fingers and change one thing to make that number go up, what would it be?
- ☐ What do you like most about your looks and what do you like least?
- ☐ Do you have a crush or have you ever been in love? If so, who is it, does that person know, and what happened to make you first notice them?
- ☐ What have you learned about yourself from this interview?
- ☐ Set a goal for next year.
- ☐ Is there anything else you'd like to talk about? Here is your chance...

EXTRA QUESTIONS

☐ Most of us have an uncomfortable or embarrassing story about when we found out how babies were made. Who told you, how did you find out, and was it awkward?

☐ If you could give yourself some advice ten years from now, what would it be? Go ahead and say it, directly into the camera to your future self.

☐ Do you drink, smoke, or do drugs? If so, what do you do and how often do you do it and who do you do it with? And, if you don't, do you think you will?

☐ What do you think people most misunderstand about you?

☐ What is your greatest worry or insecurity? What causes you to lay awake at night?

☐ Now try to go deeper... What do you think your greatest fear is in life?

☐ If there is a creator of the universe and you had the chance to ask them one question, what would it be?

☐ If you were not allowed to see your family again, what would you want them to know?

The 5000 Days Project, siblings Miles & Chantelle

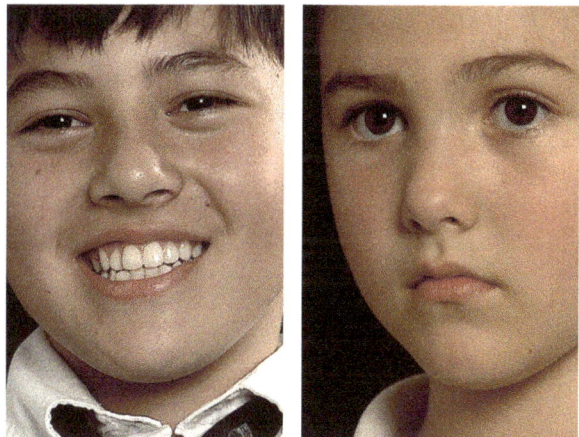

AGE 14, CORE QUESTIONS

- [ ] What is your full name and how old are you?
- [ ] Now think for a moment. On a scale of 1-10, how are you feeling today? With one meaning miserable and 10 being super happy. Tell me why you are feeling this way.
- [ ] What do you want to do when you grow up? And if you don't know, try to remove all practical considerations. What's your ultimate dream?
- [ ] What have you learned about yourself or about life this year?
- [ ] What do you think your best qualities are? I'm not talking about what you do. I'm talking about who you are.
- [ ] What do you need to work on?
- [ ] What makes you really happy? For instance, if you could spend the perfect day, what would you be doing?
- [ ] What makes you angry and why? Give an example.
- [ ] What do people most misunderstand about you?
- [ ] Have any of your friends or schoolmates ever said or done anything that hurt you or made you feel bad? What happened and what did you do?
- [ ] When was the last time you cried due to sadness and why?

- [ ] What's the most emotionally difficult thing you've ever had to face?
- [ ] Describe each member of your family using only one word for each… including yourself.
- [ ] What is the most frustrating thing about your parents/guardians? Is there something you want to do differently when you're a parent/guardian?
- [ ] What is one of your happiest childhood memories? Where were you, what were you doing, and with whom?
- [ ] If you had three wishes (and no, you can't wish for more wishes), what would you ask for?
- [ ] On a scale of 1-10, how happy are you overall?
- [ ] If you could snap your fingers and change one thing to make that number go up, what would it be?
- [ ] What do you like most about your looks and what do you like least?
- [ ] Do you have a crush or have you ever been in love? If so, who is it, does that person know, and what happened to make you first notice them?
- [ ] What have you learned about yourself from this interview?
- [ ] Set a goal for next year.
- [ ] Is there anything else you'd like to talk about? Here is your chance….

EXTRA QUESTIONS

☐ Most of us have an uncomfortable or embarrassing story about when we found out how babies were made. Who told you, how did you find out, and was it awkward?

☐ If you could give yourself some advice ten years from now, what would it be? Go ahead and say it, directly into the camera to your future self.

☐ Do you drink, smoke, or do drugs? If so, what do you do, how often do you do it, and who do you do it with? And, if you don't, do you think you will?

☐ What is your greatest worry or insecurity? What causes you to lay awake at night?

☐ Now try to go deeper... What do you think your greatest fear is in life?

☐ If there is a creator of the universe and you had the chance to ask them one question, what would it be?

☐ If you were not allowed to see your family again, what would you want them to know?

The 5000 Days Project, siblings Natassia & Max

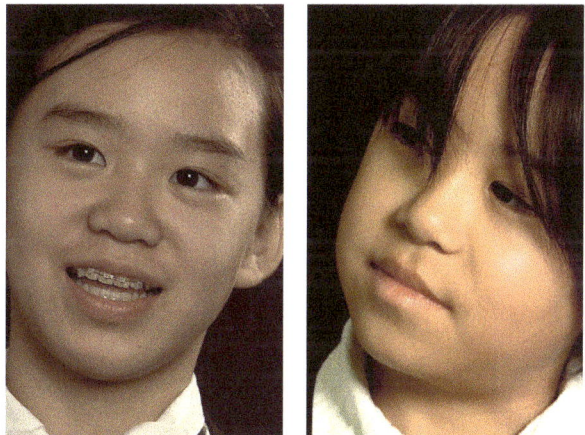

AGE 15, CORE QUESTIONS

- ☐ What is your full name and how old are you?
- ☐ Now think for a moment. On a scale of 1-10, how are you feeling today? With one meaning miserable and 10 being super happy. Tell me why you are feeling this way.
- ☐ What do you want to do when you grow up? And if you don't know, try to remove all practical considerations. What is your ultimate dream?
- ☐ What have you learned about yourself or about life this year?
- ☐ What do you think your best qualities are? I'm not talking about what you do. I'm talking about who you are.
- ☐ What do you need to work on?
- ☐ What makes you really happy? For instance, if you could spend the perfect day, what would you be doing?
- ☐ What makes you angry and why? Give an example.
- ☐ Who's your closest friend and how did you meet them?
- ☐ Have any of your friends or schoolmates ever said or done anything that hurt you or made you feel bad? What happened and what did you do?
- ☐ When is the last time you cried due to sadness and why?

- ☐ What's the most emotionally difficult thing you've ever had to face?
- ☐ Describe each member of your family using only one word for each… including yourself.
- ☐ What is the most frustrating thing about your parents/guardians? Is there something you want to do differently when you're a parent/guardian?
- ☐ What is one of your happiest childhood memories? Where were you, what were you doing and with whom?
- ☐ If you had three wishes (and no, you can't wish for more wishes), what would you wish for?
- ☐ On a scale of 1-10, how happy are you overall?
- ☐ If you could snap your fingers and change one thing to make that number go up, what would it be?
- ☐ What do you like most about your looks and what do you like least?
- ☐ Do you have a crush or have you ever been in love? If so, who is it, does that person know, and what happened to make you first notice them?
- ☐ What have you learned about yourself from this interview?
- ☐ Set a goal for next year.
- ☐ What are you most grateful for?

☐ Is there anything else you'd like to talk about? Here is your chance…

EXTRA QUESTIONS

☐ How are you with peer pressure? When is the last time you did something that you knew you should not do—but did it anyway because of your friends?

☐ Do you drink, smoke, or do drugs? If so, what do you do and how often do you do it, and who do you do it with? And, if you don't, do you think you will?

☐ What do you think people most misunderstand about you?

☐ What is your greatest worry or insecurity? What causes you to lay awake at night?

☐ Now try to go deeper… What do you think your greatest fear is in life? And I don't mean spiders. People have a fear of failure, abandonment, losing loved ones, being alone—what is your greatest fear?

☐ If there is a creator of the universe and you had the chance to ask them one question, what would it be?

☐ If you were not allowed to see your family again, what would you want them to know?

The 5000 Days Project, siblings Paloma & Beau

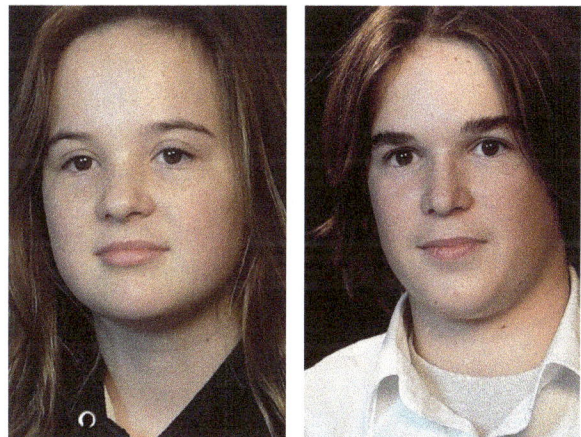

AGE 16, CORE QUESTIONS

- ☐ What is your full name and how old are you?
- ☐ Now think for a moment. On a scale of 1-10, how are you feeling today? With one meaning miserable and 10 being super happy. Tell me why you are feeling this way.
- ☐ What do you want to do when you grow up? And if you don't know, try to remove all practical considerations. What's your ultimate dream?
- ☐ What have you learned about yourself or about life this year?
- ☐ What do you think your best qualities are? I'm not talking about what you do. I'm talking about who you are.
- ☐ What do you need to work on?
- ☐ What makes you really happy? For instance, if you could spend the perfect day, what would you be doing?
- ☐ What makes you angry and why? Give an example.
- ☐ Who's your closest friend and how did you meet them?
- ☐ Have any of your friends or schoolmates ever said or done anything that hurt you or made you feel bad? What happened and what did you do?
- ☐ When is the last time you cried due to sadness and why?
- ☐ What's the most emotionally difficult thing you've ever had to face?
- ☐ Describe each member of your family using only one word for each… including yourself.
- ☐ What is the most frustrating thing about your parents/guardians? Is there something you want to do differently when you're a parent/guardian?
- ☐ What is one of your happiest childhood memories? Where were you, what were you doing, and with whom?
- ☐ If you had three wishes (and no, you can't wish for more wishes), what would you ask for?
- ☐ On a scale of 1-10, how happy are you overall?
- ☐ If you could snap your fingers and change one thing to make that number go up, what would it be?
- ☐ What do you like most about your looks and what do you like least?
- ☐ Do you have a crush or have you ever been in love? If so, who is it, does that person know, and what happened to make you first notice them?
- ☐ What have you learned about yourself from this interview?
- ☐ Set a goal for next year.
- ☐ What are you most grateful for?

☐ Is there anything else you'd like to talk about? Here is your chance….

EXTRA QUESTIONS

☐ How are you with peer pressure? When is the last time you did something that you knew you should not do—but did it anyway because of your friends?

☐ Do you drink, smoke or do drugs? If so, what do you do and how often do you do it, and who do you do it with? And, if you don't, do you think you will?

☐ What do you think people most misunderstand about you?

☐ What is your greatest worry or insecurity? What causes you to lay awake at night?

☐ Now try to go deeper... What do you think your greatest fear is in life?

☐ If there is a creator of the universe and you had the chance to ask them one question, what would it be?

☐ If you were not allowed to see your family again, what would you want them to know?

☐ What are you most grateful for?

The 5000 Days Project, siblings Canon & Ciel

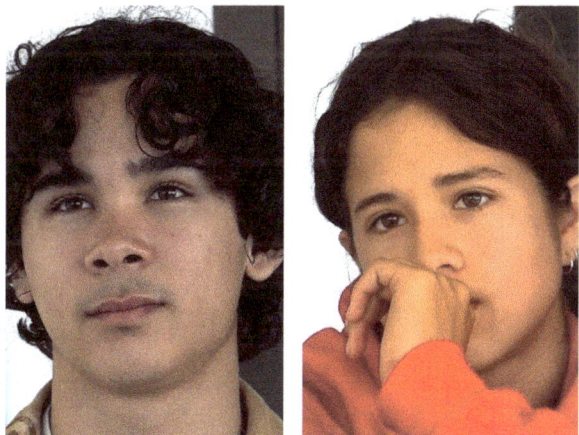

AGE 17, CORE QUESTIONS

- [ ] What is your full name and how old are you?
- [ ] Now think for a moment. On a scale of 1 -10, how are you feeling today? With one meaning miserable and 10 being super happy. Tell me why you are feeling this way.
- [ ] What do you want to do when you grow up? And are you currently doing anything to get there and, if so, what?
- [ ] What have you learned about yourself or about life this year?
- [ ] What do you think your best qualities are? I'm not talking about what you do. I'm talking about who you are.
- [ ] What do you need to work on?
- [ ] What makes you really happy? For instance, if you could spend the perfect day, what would you be doing?
- [ ] What makes you angry and why? Give an example.
- [ ] Who's your closest friend and how did you meet them?
- [ ] Have any of your friends or schoolmates ever said or done anything that hurt you or made you feel bad? What happened and what did you do?
- [ ] When is the last time you cried due to sadness and why?
- [ ] What's the most emotionally difficult thing you've ever had to face?

- [ ] Describe each member of your family using only one word for each… including yourself.
- [ ] What is the most frustrating thing about your parents/guardians? Is there something you want to do differently when you're a parent/guardian?
- [ ] What is one of your happiest childhood memories? Where were you, what were you doing, and with whom?
- [ ] If you had three wishes (and no, you can't wish for more wishes), what would you ask for?
- [ ] On a scale of 1-10, how happy are you overall?
- [ ] If you could snap your fingers and change one thing to make that number go up, what would it be?
- [ ] What do you like most about your looks and what do you like least?
- [ ] Do you have a crush or have you ever been in love? If so, who is it, does that person know, and what happened to make you first notice them?
- [ ] What have you learned about yourself from this interview?
- [ ] What are you most grateful for?
- [ ] Set a goal for next year.
- [ ] What was your goal last year? Did you accomplish it?

☐ Is there anything else you'd like to talk about? Here is your chance….

EXTRA QUESTIONS

☐ When you're older, do you want to be married and have kids? If so, how many?

☐ How are you with peer pressure? When is the last time you did something that you knew you should not do—but did it anyway because of your friends?

☐ Do you drink, smoke or do drugs? If so, what do you do and how often do you do it and who do you do it with? And, if you don't, do you think you will?

☐ What do you think people most misunderstand about you?

☐ What is your greatest worry or insecurity? What causes you to lay awake at night?

☐ Now try to go deeper... What do you think your greatest fear is in life?

☐ If there is a creator of the universe and you had the chance to ask them one question, what would it be?

☐ If you were not allowed to see your family again, what would you want them to know?

The 5000 Days Project, siblings Zara & Sienna

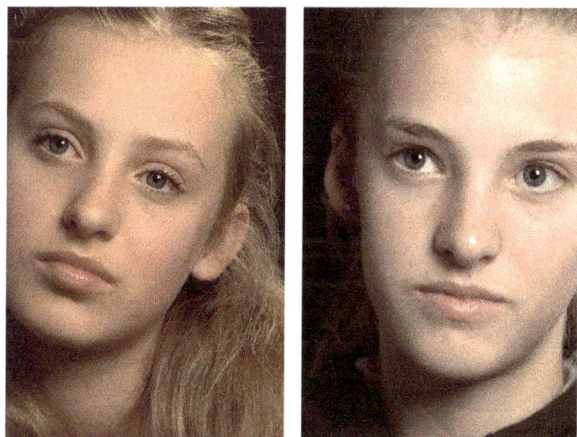

AGE 18, CORE QUESTIONS

Dr. Rick Stevenson

☐ What is your full name and how old are you?

☐ Now think for a moment. On a scale of 1-10, how are you feeling today? With one meaning miserable and 10 being super happy. Tell me why you are feeling this way.

☐ Now that you're of graduation age, what plans do you have for next year, and how do they relate to what you eventually want to do?

☐ What have you learned about yourself or about life this year?

☐ What do you think your best qualities are? I'm not talking about what you do. I'm talking about who you are.

☐ What do you need to work on?

☐ What makes you really happy? For instance, if you could spend the perfect day, what would you be doing?

☐ What makes you angry and why? Give an example.

☐ Who's your closest friend and how did you meet them?

☐ Have any of your friends or schoolmates ever said or done anything that hurt you or made you feel bad? What happened and what did you do?

☐ When was the last time you cried due to sadness and why?

☐ What's the most emotionally difficult thing you've ever had to face?

☐ Describe each member of your family using only one word for each… including yourself.

☐ What is the most frustrating thing about your parents/guardians? Is there something you want to do differently when you're a parent/guardian?

☐ What is one of your happiest childhood memories? Where were you, what were you doing, and with whom?

☐ If you had three wishes (and no, you can't wish for more wishes), what would you ask for?

☐ On a scale of 1-10, how happy are you overall?

☐ If you could snap your fingers and change one thing to make that number go up, what would it be?

☐ What do you like most about your looks and what do you like least?

☐ Do you have a crush or have you ever been in love? If so, who is it, does that person know, and what happened to make you first notice them?

☐ What have you learned about yourself from this interview?

☐ What are you most grateful for?

☐ Set a goal for next year.

- [ ] What was your goal last year? Did you accomplish it?
- [ ] Is there anything else you'd like to talk about? Here is your chance….

EXTRA QUESTIONS

- [ ] When you're older, do you want to be married and have kids? If so, how many?
- [ ] How are you with peer pressure? When is the last time you did something that you knew you should not do—but did it anyway because of your friends?
- [ ] Do you drink, smoke, or do drugs? If so, what do you do and how often do you do it, and who do you do it with? And, if you don't, do you think you will?
- [ ] What do you think people most misunderstand about you?
- [ ] What is your greatest worry or insecurity? What causes you to lay awake at night?
- [ ] Now try to go deeper... What do you think your greatest fear is in life?
- [ ] If there is a creator of the universe and you had the chance to ask them one question, what would it be?
- [ ] If you were not allowed to see your family again, what would you want them to know?
- [ ] What do you want to know most about your future?

The 5000 Days Project, siblings Riyad & Kayden

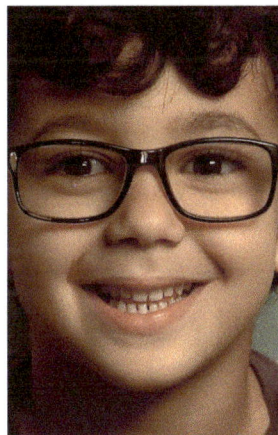

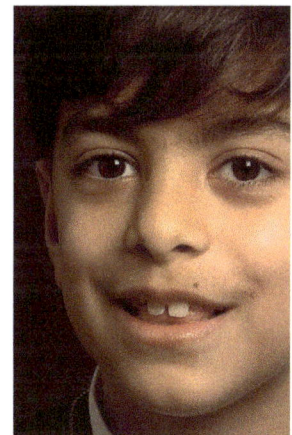

TAKING STOCK & LEGACY CLASSIC INTERVIEWS

Taking Stock and Legacy Classic are interviews designed for people of all ages who want to check in on their lives and create a time capsule for the future. They help capture the story they were born into, where they currently are in life, and what their hopes and dreams are for the future. The process is meant to help them connect the dots of their lives, put their past and future in perspective, and look to identify those things that might be holding them back from being the best version of who they are.

The key to giving a StoryQ Taking Stock or Legacy Classic interview lies with the humility and courage of the interviewer. Many of these people will be highly accomplished and some will be older so Personal Story Mentoring should be approached with humility. We are facilitators or tour guides exploring the story of their lives. We are not there to instruct. We are there to hold a mirror up to the individual and hold it steady enough that they can clearly see themselves.

There are two ultimate goals. First, the interview should give them perspective on themselves and their lives. As I've said before, we often live our lives as if we're standing in front of a 100 foot-painting of ourselves yet we are only one foot away. We only see a small part of ourselves—more often just the flaws

Watch our short film on Coach Dar's Taking Stock interview.

tinyurl.com/storyq19

and brush strokes. But what happens when we step back? We get the full picture. The interviewer should be there to enable the "step back."

Second, not unlike the 5000 Days Project interviews, we hope that questions will lead to revelations that can not only give the individual a new perspective, but help them identify and heal their pain points. All of us have blindspots where our bodies and minds are inefficiently struggling with some past trauma or current anxiety.

Just as you listen to a broken engine for "clanks" to find where the break is so you can fix it, you have to look for clues that will help address things that are making their lives less than they can be. Of course, many of us deal with pain by trying to block it rather than dealing with the source. This is what leads to substance abuse and other forms of pain relief which of course can result in a whole other set of problems.

DIFFERENCES BETWEEN TAKING STOCK AND LEGACY CLASSIC

The questions are basically the same so what is the difference between conducting a Legacy Classic interview and a Taking Stock interview? If the interviewee is in their later years, the Legacy Classic interview focuses primarily on the past and our goal is to help capture their story primarily for their family. Legacy Classic is for the individual who is conscious of nearing the end of their life and wants to pass on final thoughts to those they love. Beyond giving them the chance to say things that have gone unsaid or express their final peace, the question selection is the same. Only the intent and gravity are different. Hence, select the questions that best serve that need.

Conversely, Taking Stock is a forward-looking yet reflective interview process distinctively different from a life-encompassing legacy interview. I've interviewed people nearing their nineties who are just as anxious to look forward as younger adults, so the appropriate choice of interviews depends upon the subject. Again, select the questions that best serve that need.

Knowing that the humility of the interviewer is the key, the questions are organized in a way to allow the interviewee to slowly discover themselves in an unthreatening way. As with the interviews for kids, it is still key to capture the interviewee's longings and fears as well as their character arc—their main struggle to overcome. However, the road to those revelations is more apt to emerge through their past influences as revealed in their stories. Hence, the questions you will want to ask to create their time capsule may lead you down rabbit holes. Follow them.

Childhood, Adult and Family Relationships, Faith, Career, Mentors. All provide opportunities for exploration. You won't get to all of them and maybe to no more than a third of them, so pick and choose based on what seems to be opening the doors.

The World View and Reflection questions include the big ones, so make those your ultimate priority. After the interviewee has gained some perspective on past influences, they can draw some important conclusions and share some vital wisdom from this list. Many people truly feel like they have very little to share of value. That comes from both humility and lack of perspective. The best response is: let's let the future be the judge of that. As I've mentioned, Tolkien metaphorically viewed all of humankind as a giant choir which only reaches sonic perfection when *every* voice can be heard. I agree.

I was interviewing a highly successful yet extremely modest 87-year-old man recently who believed he had nothing of value to say even though his life has influenced thousands of others. In a wavering moment he asked, "Now, why am I doing this again?" I replied, "Well there are many reasons but the one that really counts is that you're doing it because you love your daughter." That was enough for him. It's up to us to ask, beg, or even bribe our parents and friends to record their stories and then it's up to them to leave that story—the most valuable things they'll each own—as their contribution to their family and the universe.

Use this QR code for a Legacy interview conducted by a student story mentor

tinyurl.com/storyq20

TAKING STOCK & LEGACY CORE QUESTIONS

- ☐ What is your full name, and when and where were you born?
- ☐ What were your nicknames, and how do you feel about them?
- ☐ What is your earliest memory, and what emotion do you associate with it? (Explore that initial POV of the world and see if and how it has informed their world view.)
- ☐ Describe each member of your birth family using only one or two words each. (Explore anything illuminating.)
- ☐ Growing up, which member were you closest to and why?
- ☐ What did your parents do for a living, and what role did money play in your family?
- ☐ What is the most valuable lesson you learned from your parents?
- ☐ What was one of your favorite things to do as a kid? What made you happy?
- ☐ What did you get in trouble for most as a kid?
- ☐ What was one of the most difficult challenges you had to face growing up?
- ☐ How did it contribute to who you've become?
- ☐ As a kid, what did you want to do when you grew up, and how did it relate to what you eventually did for your career?

ADULT & FAMILY RELATIONSHIP QUESTIONS

- ☐ (Assuming marriage or significant relationship) When and how did you meet your partner?
- ☐ (Assuming family) Describe each member of your current family with one or two words.
- ☐ Are any of your greatest current struggles or worries tied to those relationships?
- ☐ (Assuming children) Describe each child. What was your proudest moment as a parent?
- ☐ What is one of your favorite family stories to tell?

FAITH OR BELIEF SYSTEM

- ☐ Did church or faith play a role in your life and, if so, how?
- ☐ Have you ever witnessed what you consider to be a miracle? If so, explain.
- ☐ Where do you think we go when we die?
- ☐ (Assuming there is a God) If you could ask God one question, what would you ask? What do you want to know?

CAREER

- ☐ Talk about your career journey, the path you took and where you have ended up so far.
- ☐ What was your darkest moment, and what was your proudest moment?

☐ What did you learn from both?

MENTORS
☐ What person or persons had the most positive impact on your life?
☐ Do you have mentees, and what is the most important thing you would want them to know before you die?

WORLD VIEW AND REFLECTIONS (OVERVIEW)
☐ What is your greatest personal struggle at the moment, and what does its successful conclusion look like?
☐ On a scale of 1-10 with 10 being the happiest, how happy are you?
☐ If you could snap your fingers and change one thing to make that number go up, what would it be?
☐ If you could do one thing differently or change an event or decision in your life, what would it be and why?
☐ Alternately, as you look back at your life, what were the one or two tipping points or moments of truth that had the greatest impact on your life?
☐ If we are all a product of our longings and our fears, what has been your greatest longing and what is your greatest fear?

☐ If we all live on a continuum between our longings and our fears, where do you live—closer to your longings or closer to your fears?
☐ How has that affected your world view? Do you see the world in abundance or deficit, as a cup half-empty or a cup half-full?
☐ If you could pass on one bit of life advice to the world, what would it be?
☐ You've been writing your resume for years. Now, if you could write your epitaph, what would it say?
☐ If this were your last day on Earth and you wanted to say something to your loved ones, what would it be?
☐ If you could live one day or event over again, which one would it be and why?
☐ What are you most grateful for?
☐ What plans are you most excited about going forward, in your next act?
☐ Is there anything else you would like to add to this?

Ages 19 through 99 obviously represent a wide range. While the Taking Stock and Legacy Classic interviews provide a good framework for all adult interviews, you may wish to draw on some age and circumstance-specific questions to customize your interview as required.

QUESTIONS FOR COLLEGE/UNIVERSITY STUDENTS

- [ ] What is your full name, how old are you, and where are you from?
- [ ] What do you want to do when you finish your degree?
- [ ] Answer that question again now without any practical restrictions. If you could do anything when your studies are completed, what would it be?
- [ ] What was your greatest fear coming here and what has been the biggest surprise?
- [ ] What have you learned about yourself since arriving at college?
- [ ] What do you most enjoy doing? What makes you happy?
- [ ] Who or what do you care about the most?
- [ ] What really annoys you or makes you angry?
- [ ] When is the last time you cried and why?
- [ ] What's the most emotionally painful thing that has ever happened to you?
- [ ] Throughout your life, what has been your greatest fear (e.g., commitment, abandonment, failure, success)?
- [ ] According to studies, loneliness is the most common emotion felt by first-year college students. How often do you feel this way and how do you cope with it?
- [ ] Do you think people get you? If not, what do you think they most misunderstand about you?

- [ ] What do you like most and least about your appearance?
- [ ] What tendency of yours gets you in the most trouble or works against your long term goals and how has it affected your life here?
- [ ] What's your happiest childhood memory?
- [ ] Describe each member of your family using only one word for each—including yourself.
- [ ] Rate yourself in terms of happiness this year on a scale of 1-10 with 10 being the happiest.
- [ ] If you could change one thing to make your life better, what would it be?
- [ ] Are you in love or attracted to someone and, if so, what are you doing about it?
- [ ] Describe your perfect future 10 years from now. Where would you live? What would you be doing? Would you have a family?
- [ ] From a global perspective, what are you most concerned about and, if you had the means, how would you deal with it?
- [ ] If you had three wishes (and no you cannot have a genie nor more wishes), what would you wish for?
- [ ] What are you most grateful for?
- [ ] Is there anything else you'd like to talk about? Here is your chance....

QUESTIONS FOR YOUNG ADULTS

☐ What compliments do you frequently receive?

☐ What is the biggest risk you've ever taken? Was it worth it?

☐ If you could instantly change one thing about yourself, what would it be?

☐ Tell me a story about yourself that reveals who you are.

☐ Tell me about a time that you've failed. What did you learn, and how did it change you?

☐ What are you passionate about?

☐ When do you feel like you became an adult? Or have you felt that yet?

☐ If you could spend a week with any historical figure, who would it be and why?

☐ Tell me about a conversation you've had that changed your perspective.

☐ What is your favorite and least favorite personal characteristic?

☐ What is your favorite quotation and why?

StoryQ Personal Story Mentor Max Losee

QUESTIONS FOR YOUNG COUPLES

- ☐ What is your name and age, and with whom are you in a relationship?
- ☐ When and how did you meet?
- ☐ How and when did you know you were in love?
- ☐ What most endeared or attracted you to them?
- ☐ What do you think most attracted or endeared them to you?
- ☐ What fears or concerns did you initially have about them?
- ☐ How did you overcome those concerns? Did you accept them, ignore them, or count on them changing?
- ☐ Did they change or did you change? Describe.
- ☐ What action or event caused the relationship to go to the next level?
- ☐ Do you share the same values or do you differ in certain areas?
- ☐ Do you share the same politics and, if not, how do you differ?
- ☐ Do you think it's okay to keep looking at members of the opposite sex once you're in a relationship?
- ☐ What most bugs you about your partner?
- ☐ What do you trust the most about your partner?
- ☐ Do you feel secure or insecure in your relationship? Why?
- ☐ What do you want or need most from this relationship, and are you getting it?
- ☐ What does your significant other want or need from you, and are they getting it?
- ☐ What is the thing that your partner misunderstands most about you?
- ☐ Can you tell your partner the truth about yourself?
- ☐ On a Scale of 1-10, how well do you think you know your partner, with 10 being the highest?
- ☐ On a Scale of 1-10 with 10 being the happiest, how happy are you?
- ☐ How could you be happier? What changes would you need to make?
- ☐ How does faith, religion, or God figure into your relationship?
- ☐ On a Scale of 1-10, how physically attracted were you to your partner when you met? What traits did you find attractive?
- ☐ Physically speaking, what do you think they were most drawn to in you?
- ☐ On a Scale of 1-10, how attracted are you to your partner today?
- ☐ What are you most fearful of or do you worry about most in the relationship?
- ☐ Do you see yourself spending the rest of your life with this person?
- ☐ When you fight, how are disagreements generally resolved?

- ☐ What defenses do you put up that get in the way of connecting with the other person?
- ☐ What sort of defenses do they put up that get in the way of connecting with you?
- ☐ Do you or your partner withhold affection? If so, when and how?
- ☐ How do you show your love for your partner?
- ☐ How have you changed since being with your partner? Are you happy with these changes or unhappy? Explain.
- ☐ Make three wishes for the relationship, anything you want....
- ☐ Do you consider this person your best friend? Why so or not?
- ☐ Are you the type of partner you'd like to have as a partner?
- ☐ What are you most grateful for in the other person?

QUESTIONS ABOUT SEX (OPTIONAL)

- ☐ How would you rate your sex life on a scale of 1-10? How could it be better?
- ☐ Does your partner know how you feel?
- ☐ Can you talk to your partner about these things?

StoryQ Founder Dr. Rick Stevenson

Use this QR code to learn more about StoryQ founder Dr. Rick Stevenson.

tinyurl.com/storyq21

FAMILY QUESTIONS FOR INTERACTIVE GROUP INTERVIEWS

☐ From youngest to oldest, introduce yourselves, giving your names and ages.

☐ Starting with the oldest, describe the next -youngest family member using just one word!

☐ Share one of your best family memories. Where were you, what were you doing, and what made it special?

☐ Share a sad family memory.

☐ Share a time when another member of the family did something extraordinarily kind for you.

☐ If you could wish one thing for your family, what would it be? And no, you can't wish for more wishes.

☐ What are you most grateful for?

☐ What makes your family unique, or special?

☐ Share a favorite memory about one of your ancestors... a grandparent, or perhaps great-grandparent.

☐ Is there anything you'd like to share or add for your first family journal? Go ahead and share that now.

OPTIONAL SPIRITUAL QUESTIONS

Customize the following for the faith system of your interviewee.

FOR AGES 4-9

☐ What do you think God looks like?

☐ What is your favorite Bible (or Quran, or…) story and why?

☐ If you could ask God any question, what would you ask Him?

FOR AGES 10 AND UP

☐ When do you feel closest to God?

☐ How often do you pray and what do you pray for?

☐ On a scale of 1-10 with 10 being the highest, where would you rate your faith and what could you do to improve it?

☐ How does your faith in God influence your everyday thoughts and actions? Give examples.

QUESTIONS FOR DAILY JOURNALING

- ☐ What is the best thing that's happened to you lately?
- ☐ What's the worst thing that's happened?
- ☐ What's your greatest challenge right now? How are you doing with it?
- ☐ Think about all of your relationships. Are there one or more that are causing you to be frustrated or sad? If so, which ones, and why?
- ☐ What can you do to repair or heal things?
- ☐ If knowledge is power and self-knowledge is superpower, what are you learning about yourself in terms of what you really want or care about—and in terms of what you fear?
- ☐ How do your fears hold you back from being who you want to be?
- ☐ Set a goal for this coming week.
- ☐ Set a goal for this coming year.
- ☐ What are you most grateful for?

QUESTIONS FOR EDUCATORS

- ☐ What is your favorite thing to do when you don't have to do anything?
- ☐ What is the most important thing for others to know about you?
- ☐ Think of an educator you've had who made a difference in your life. What were the qualities of that person that affected you?
- ☐ Besides the desire for fame and fortune, what happened to make you want to become an educator?
- ☐ How has your experience thus far met or exceeded your expectations?
- ☐ How does who you are in your deepest truth match with what you do in your job?
- ☐ How long have you been in education? What is the greatest change you've noticed in your career?
- ☐ What are your strengths as an educator?
- ☐ What is a challenging situation you've had with a student—one that you wish you had handled more effectively?
- ☐ What is an important lesson you've learned that you would want to pass on to those new to the profession?
- ☐ What is an emotionally challenging event that happened in your classroom experience?

- ☐ What is a meaningful event that has happened in the classroom that has stayed with you?
- ☐ If you could change one thing to improve the educational system what would it be?
- ☐ What is your greatest worry, insecurity or fear about your job? Does anything in particular cause you to lay awake at night?
- ☐ If you had three teacher wishes (and no you cannot ask for more wishes) what would you wish for?

Use the QR codes below to watch more stories generated from the decades of Personal Story Mentoring interviews conducted by Dr. Rick Steveson.

Watch this 60+ minute uncut interview with Jack Robinson.

tinyurl.com/sqmed01

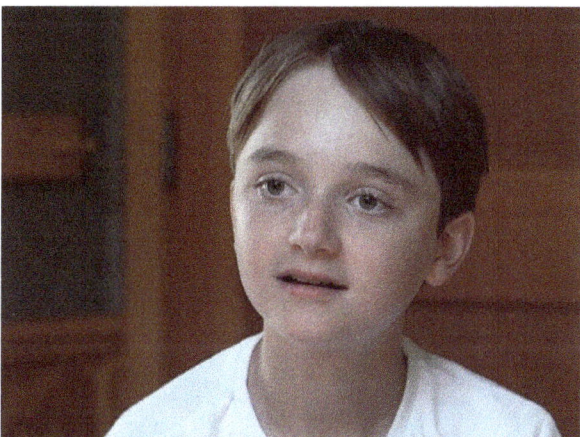

Cormac Thompson shares his musical story with Rick in *A Borrowed Gift*.

tinyurl.com/sqmed02

This moving 10-minute story about body image features Nicki Cox.

tinyurl.com/sqmed03

Dr. Rick Stevenson

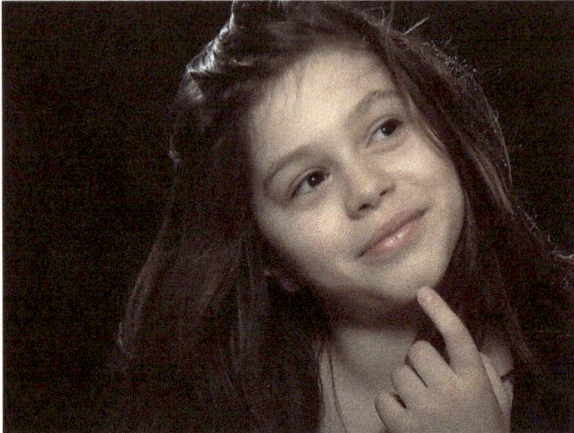

Over the years, Rachel ponders what *Grown Up* means to her.

tinyurl.com/sqmed04

Briton Vijay grapples with identity in this Prodigy Camp film.

tinyurl.com/sqmed05

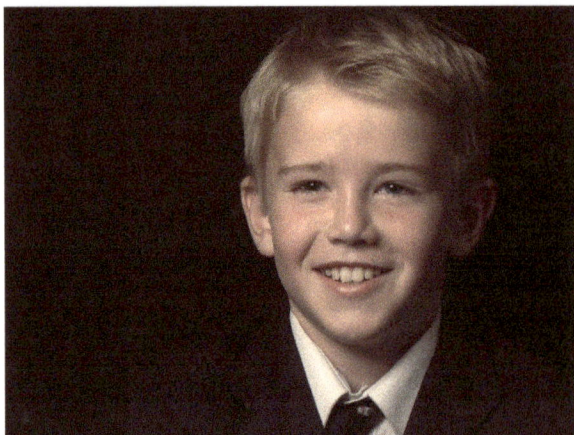

Sam doesn't want to grow up, but life takes him to unexpected places.

tinyurl.com/sqmed06

Zara resists her dreams about the future, but they find her anyway.

tinyurl.com/sqmed07

Sam struggles with ADD but finds his genius in mechanics.

tinyurl.com/sqmed08

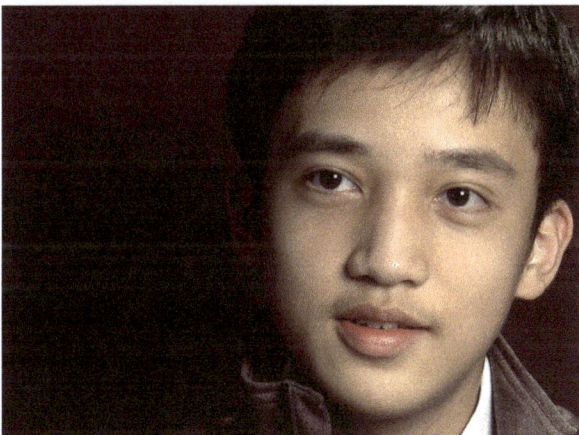

Alden learns that limiting work in favor of living life is the real achievement.

tinyurl.com/sqmed09

Dr. Rick Stevenson

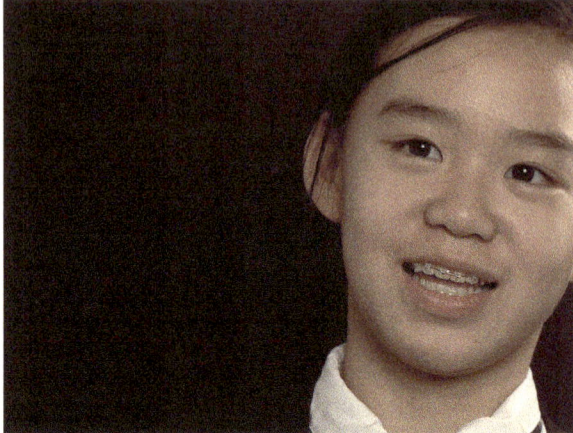

Natassia struggles to be heard, then finds her voice.

tinyurl.com/sqmed10

Jack is bright and gregarious but struggles with change and injustice.

tinyurl.com/sqmed11

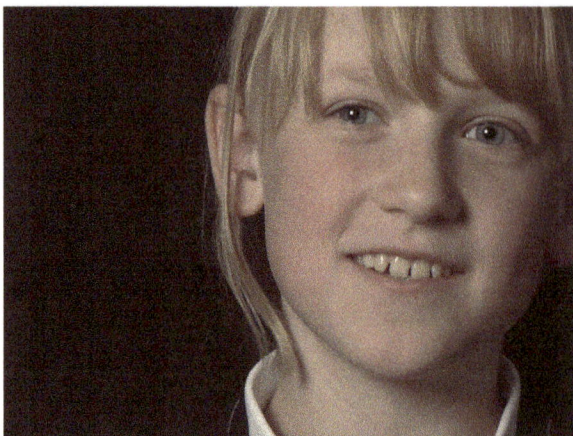

Addy wants to be an inventor... and finds she has to re-invent herself.

tinyurl.com/sqmda12

Henry is a perfectionist but discovers beauty in imperfection.

tinyurl.com/sqmed13

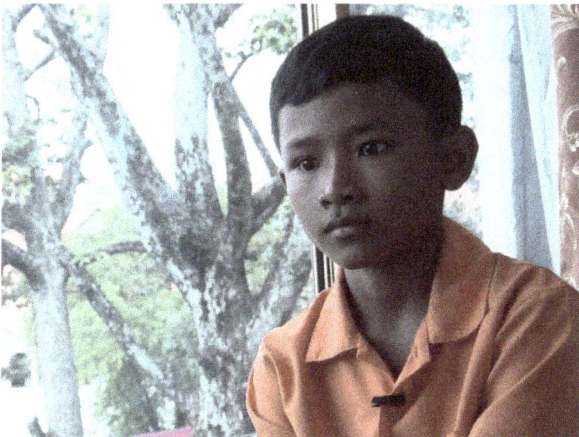

Sophea's story is one of the exploration of feelings about loss.

tinyurl.com/sqmed14

Rick filmed this tribute to Nakota, who passed away far too young.

tinyurl.com/sqmed15

Dr. Rick Stevenson

Watch this trailer for StoryQ's Taking Stock series of interviews.

tinyurl.com/sqmed16

Taking Stock interview with Dune Thorne, Invest in Girls founder.

tinyurl.com/sqmed17

Taking Stock interview with Gerald Gangaram, US Army Apache pilot.

tinyurl.com/sqmed18

Watch this trailer promoting the early days of the 5000 Days Project.

tinyurl.com/sqmed19

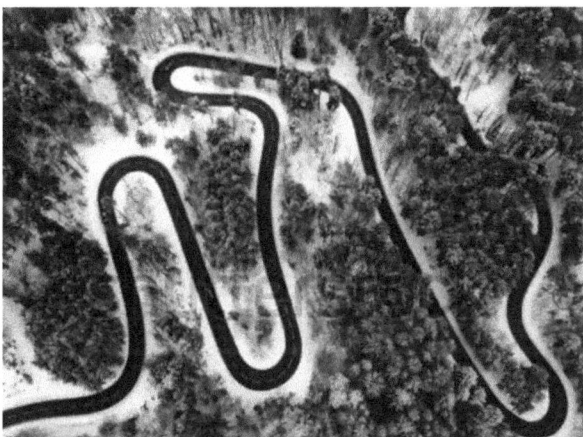

The Roadmap of Adolescence explains the importance of perspective.

tinyurl.com/sqmed20

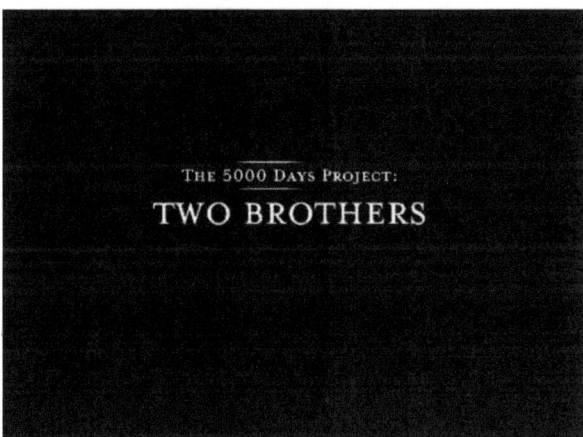

THE 5000 DAYS PROJECT:
TWO BROTHERS

This was the first feature-length film produced by The 5000 Days Project.

tinyurl.com/sqmed21

Jonathan | age 26

Gennette | age 25

Gwenth | age 16

Millennials Ep. 1, "Secrets," features Jade, Danielle, & Jonathan.

tinyurl.com/sqmed22

Millennials Ep. 2, "Popularity," tracks Kellan, Simon, & Gennette.

tinyurl.com/sqmed23

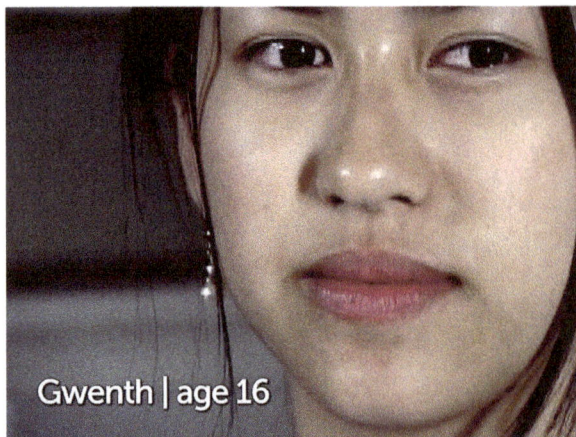

In *Millennials* Ep. 3, the "Immigrants" are Gwenth, Cristian, & Prottush.

tinyurl.com/sqmed24

Zoriah | age 21

Millennials Ep. 4 is "Siblings": Zoriah/Veda, Zeke/Eli, & Sam/Luke.

tinyurl.com/sqmda25

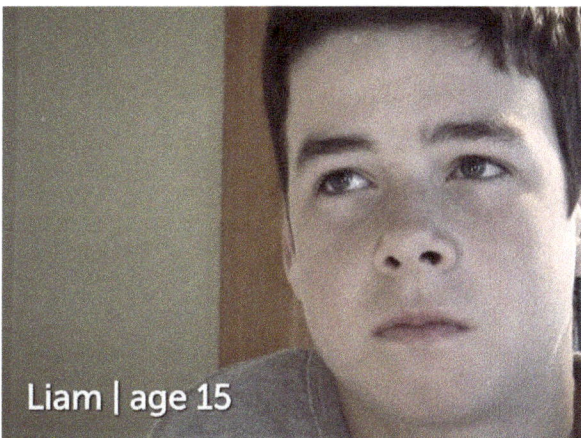

Liam | age 15

The *Millennials* Ep. 5 "Achievers" are Brittany, Liam, Haley, & Jonathan.

tinyurl.com/sqmed26

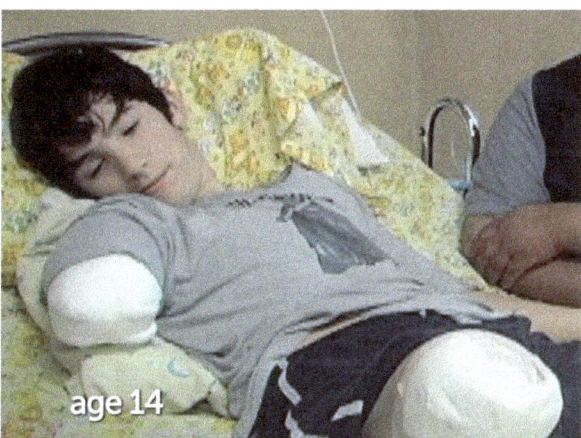

age 14

Millennials Ep. 6, "Resilience," features Luciano, Hans, & Darius.

tinyurl.com/sqmed27

Use the QR codes on the following pages to purchase a selection of books recommended by StoryQ founder Dr. Rick Stevenson.

21 Things You Forgot About Being a Kid

Dr. Rick Stevenson
5KD Publishers, 2019
tinyurl.com/storyq29

Brain Rules

John Medina
Pear Press, 2014
tinyurl.com/storyq30

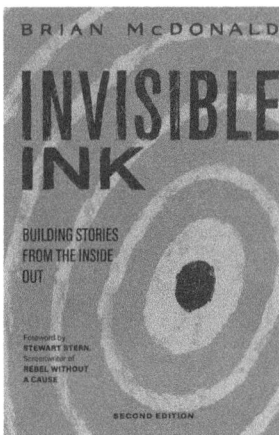

Invisible Ink

Brian McDonald
Talking Drum, 2024
tinyurl.com/storyq31

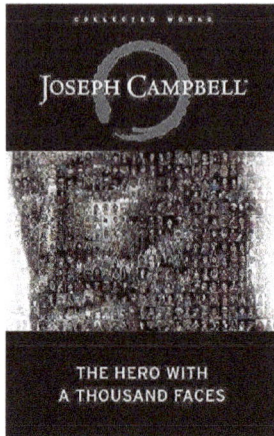

The Hero with a Thousand Faces

Joseph Campbell
New World Library, 3rd ed. 2008
tinyurl.com/storyq32

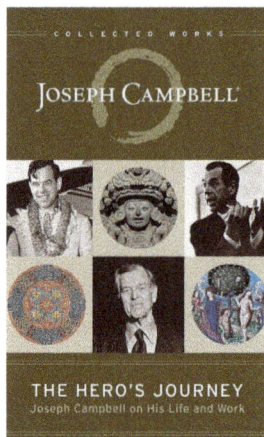

The Hero's Journey

Joseph Campbell
New World Library, 3rd ed. 2003
tinyurl.com/storyq33

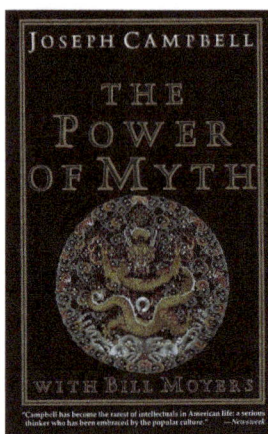

The Power of Myth

Joseph Campbell
Anchor, 1991
tinyurl.com/storyq34

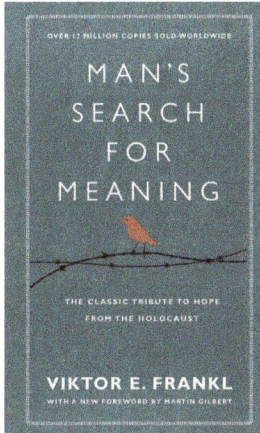

Man's Search for Meaning

Viktor E. Frankl
Rider, 2011
tinyurl.com/storyq35

Save the Cat!

Blake Snyder
Michael Wiese Productions, 2013
tinyurl.com/storyq36

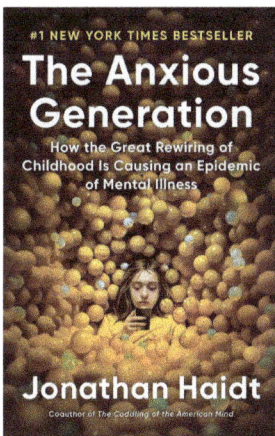

The Anxious Generation

Jonathan Haidt
Penguin Press, 2024
tinyurl.com/storyq37

IMAGE/PHOTO CREDITS

CREATIVE COMMONS AND LIST OF LICENSES

The licenses referenced in the above citations are listed below, along with the relevant URLs for license details. Any license so referenced is likewise extended by StoryQ to readers.

Creative Commons: https://en.wikipedia.org/wiki/en:Creative_Commons
Attribution 2.0 Generic: https://creativecommons.org/licenses/by/2.0/deed.en
Attribution-Share Alike 2.5 Generic: https://creativecommons.org/licenses/by-sa/2.5/deed.en
Attribution-Share Alike 3.0 Unported: https://creativecommons.org/licenses/by-sa/3.0/deed.en
Attribution-Share Alike 4.0 International: https://creativecommons.org/licenses/by-sa/4.0/deed.en
Attribution 4.0 International: https://creativecommons.org/licenses/by/4.0/deed.en
CC0 1.0 Universal Public Domain Dedication: https://creativecommons.org/publicdomain/zero/1.0/deed.en
GNU Free Documentation License, Version 1.2: https://www.gnu.org/licenses/old-licenses/fdl-1.2.en.html

OTHER IMAGES IN THIS WORK

Other images in this work are the sole property of StoryQ, are fully protected under United States Copyright Law, and used herein by permission of the image subject(s).

COLOPHON

How to Be a Personal Story Mentor:
Helping People Connect the Dots of Their Lives Using the StoryQ Method
by Dr. Rick Stevenson
was set in Minion Pro by Methow Press.
Interior Layout is by Christian Loubek, with Greg Wright.

Title Font: Bebas Neue
Subtitle Font: Gloucester MT Extra Condensed
Titlepage Author Credit: Baskerville
Chapter and Section Titles: Bebas Neue
Marginal Text: Calluna
Captions: Advent Pro

The cover design is by Christian Loubek.